LIGHTHOUSE
Legacies

Stories of Nova Scotia's Lightkeeping Families

CHRIS MILLS

NIMBUS
PUBLISHING

Nimbus Publishing Limited
PO Box 9166, Halifax, NS   B3K 5M8
(902) 455-4286

Printed and bound in Canada
Design: Troy Cole – Envision Graphic Design

Front cover: Back Row (L to R): Catherine and Edward Gallagher, Marge Williams. Front Row: Max, Ken, Don and Ed Gallagher.
Author photo: Anne Mills

Library and Archives Canada Cataloguing in Publication

Mills, Chris, 1964-
Lighthouse legacies : stories of Nova Scotia's lightkeeping families / Chris Mills
Includes bibliographical references and index.
ISBN 10: 1-55109-561-0
ISBN 13: 978-1-55109-561-5

1. Lighthouse keepers—Nova Scotia. I. Title.
VK1139.M54 2006   387.1'55'09716
C2006-901492-2

ACKNOWLEDGEMENTS

Quotations from *Keepers of the Light* and *Lights of the Inside Passage*, copyright Donald Graham, in Chapter 2 appear with the permission of Harbour Publishing Ltd.

Quotations from *We Keep A Light*, *B was for Butter* and *Enemy Craft* throughout the book appear courtesy of Betty June Smith and Anne Wickens.

Quotation from *Lost Sounds* in Chapter 7 appears with the permission of Alan Renton.

Quotations from *Rockbound* in Chapter 6 appear with the permission of the University of Toronto Press.

Quotations from *Women of the Lights* in Chapter 4 appear with the permission of Candace Fleming.

Excerpts from *It Was Fun While It Lasted* in Chapters 1 and 10 used by kind permission of Arthur Lane.

Canada

The Canada Council | Le Conseil des Arts
for the Arts | du Canada

We acknowledge the financial support of the Government of Canada through the Book Publishing Industry Development Program (BPIDP) and the Canada Council, and of the Province of Nova Scotia through the Department of Tourism, Culture and Heritage for our publishing activities.

To Maris Lilliana

and

to the memory of
Donald Wickerson Lent
(1919–2005)

Table of Contents

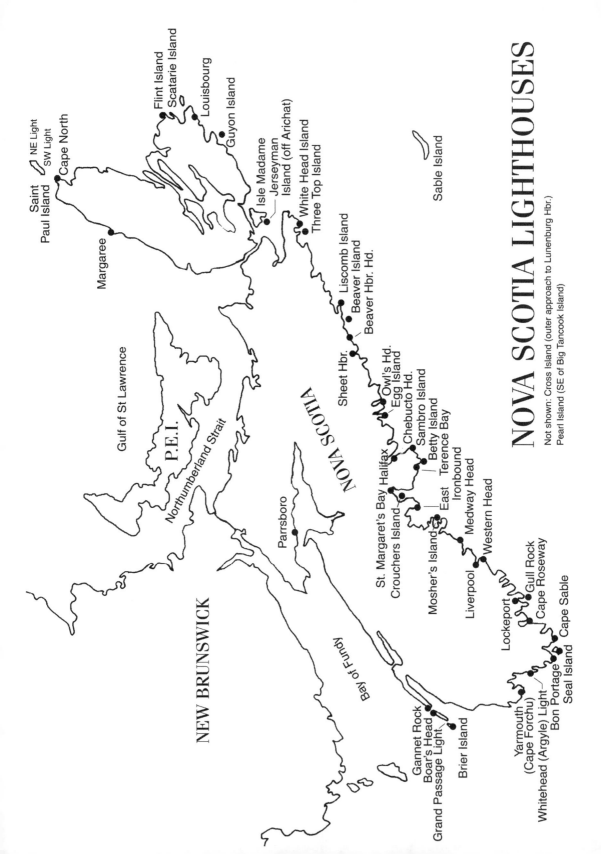

NOVA SCOTIA LIGHTHOUSES

Not shown: Cross Island (outer approach to Lunenburg Hbr.)
Pearl Island (SE of Big Tancook Island)

NEW BRUNSWICK

NOVA SCOTIA

P.E.I.

Gulf of St Lawrence

Northumberland Strait

Bay of Fundy

Saint Paul Island
NE Light
SW Light
Cape North

Margaree

Flint Island
Scatarie Island
Louisbourg
Guyon Island

Isle Madame
Jerseyman Island (off Arichat)
White Head Island
Three Top Island

Sable Island

Liscomb Island
Beaver Island
Beaver Hbr. Hd.

Sheet Hbr.

Owl's Hd.
Egg Island
Chebucto Hd.
Sambro Island
Betty Island
Terence Bay
Ironbound
Medway Head
Western Head

St. Margaret's Bay Halifax
Crouchers Island

Mosher's Island

East

Liverpool

Lockeport
Gull Rock
Cape Roseway
Cape Sable

Parrsboro

Yarmouth (Cape Forchu)
Whitehead (Argyle) Light
Bon Portage
Seal Island

Gannet Rock
Boar's Head
Grand Passage Light
Brier Island

Preface

LIGHTHOUSES ARE A RELIC OF THE PAST

IN AN AGE WHEN SATELLITE TECHNOLOGY CAN LEAD a mariner to within three feet or less of a buoy in the middle of the ocean, the practical need for a guiding light is pretty well gone. Most mariners don't rely on lighthouses much anymore. Cash-strapped governments don't want to maintain them. This is certainly the case in Canada, where the feds are now in the process of getting out of the traditional-aids-to-navigation business.

The end result is that lighthouses, already much altered by modernization, automation and neglect, are disappearing. And with them go the lifetimes of experience of hundreds of lightkeepers and their families—the very heartbeat of our guiding lights.

When I first got involved in lighthouse preservation more than a decade ago, I thought it would be a noble and wonderful thing to physically save the structures. What better way to spend a life than swinging a hammer and wielding a paintbrush to resurrect a proud sentinel of the sea? I still think it's a great idea, but in my case, it would likely mean financial destitution, divorce, and very little personal life other than saving lighthouses. So, my goal is to try to save the memories of the people who lived the lighthouse life. Their experiences are as important as the physical structures they maintained, and their memories are as endangered as the lights they once kept.

We're at a critical point in lighthouse history in Canada as the old-timers die off. In another decade or so, there won't be many people who know just what it was like to climb inside a glittering Fresnel lens, set a match to a kerosene vapour light, or stand on the spokes of a huge flywheel to start a foghorn engine.

This was the work and the life that sustained thousands of keepers and their families, beginning in 1734, when Canada's first lightkeeper lit the cod liver oil lamp in the great stone tower at Louisbourg, Cape Breton. In Nova Scotia the age of the lightkeeper ended 259 years later, when the last guardians locked up the Cape Forchu light in Yarmouth.

Cross Island, NS, in February 1989, a few months before the last keepers left.

In the fall of 1993, just months after Yarmouth's light lost its keepers, I began to interview former lightkeepers and their families as a way of saving their memories from the scourge of automation and mortality. In 2000 I picked up the pace, spurred by the obituaries in the newspaper and by an almost frantic desire to save all that I could of a vanishing way of life.

Some interviewees were friends I had made while I worked as a lightkeeper. Others I met for the first time after tracking them down through phonebooks, local knowledge, and chance encounters.

What emerged from my interviews with these folks was a remarkable series of vignettes of a life now relegated to memory and the occasional article in a newspaper or magazine. As I talked with people, I began to see patterns in their experiences, despite different family backgrounds and life on different lightstations. I decided to run with what I had, arranging stories thematically as a way of exploring lighthouse work and life.

The bulk of the interviews cover the period from 1930 to the mid-1980s. Although it seems like a short period of time, that half-century represents almost 250 years of lightkeeping experience; the way of life and the job did not change appreciably until the 1960s, when electrification made life easier—and heralded the end of the lightkeeper.

Some people were reluctant to be interviewed, at first. "Oh, I don't know anything about the history of the light! What if I can't answer your question? I'm not gonna be on camera, am I?"

Evelyn Richardson's daughter Anne Wickens wrote me that she would not necessarily be "a good candidate for a tape recording. Technical, mechanical and electronic contraptions are *anathema maranatha* to me, and put me off stride."

But Anne rose to the occasion, sitting for two sessions in front of the mic, arms folded, eyes closed and full of memories of life on Bon Portage Island.

Sometimes I interviewed two or three family members at one time, making for lively conversation as daughters corrected fathers and siblings ribbed each other about goings-on in the old days. These sessions were a nightmare to transcribe, but they are all the more important for their interaction and vitality.

I couldn't use every lighthouse story in the book. It's not for lack of wanting to, but I had so much material that I had to be careful to avoid repetition. (How many times did I hear a keeper or family member say they'd only listen for their foghorn when it *stopped* blowing?!)

I tried to stay away from a lot of purely technical questions during my interviews. It's not that I'm not interested in how the lights were built or what kinds of equipment were used. I'm as keen as the next lighthouse nut to talk about the virtues of a third-order Barbier lens over an APRB-252 plastic light.

But I think it's more important to know how people felt about lighthouse life. Humans were the heart and soul of the lighthouse. Why did they do it? What did they enjoy about it? Who hated it and why?

How did they cope with isolation, death, and routine as they lived out their lives on tiny islands and headlands?

This is what I explore in the following chapters. The book is divided into ten sections covering what I think are some of the essential themes of lightkeeping in Nova Scotia. I've also drawn from my own lightkeeping experiences in other provinces and used records from New Brunswick, Ontario and British Columbia. Despite some regional differences, keepers across Canada went through similar trials and tribulations to keep their lights burning.

The stories you'll read in this book are poignant, sad, funny, and evocative. For the most part, they are the memories of folks who loved their way of life and who continue to count it as a major influence on their outlook and personalities, even though many haven't lived at a lighthouse for decades.

Already, half a dozen of my interviewees have died, and it is a bittersweet thing to listen to my tapes and know that those voices are now silent. But those recorded voices are that much louder and more permanent now. Many will come to life again in this book.

I recorded the interviews with a standard broadcast quality Electro-Voice 635A mic—tough enough to hammer nails with—and a digital mini-disc recorder. The transcribed interviews, to date, contain about half a million words. For clarity and lack of repetition in the book, I have taken out the "ahhs" and "ums," and any redundant material. Other than that, the words you read are straight from the mouths of my interviewees. I take full responsibility for any errors in fact or context.

A note about place names: Nova Scotians and Maritimers in general tend to add an apostrophe and an *s* to local places. For example, on a nautical chart, the little speck between Black Point and French Village in St. Margaret's Bay is denoted "Croucher Island." But for anyone living in the area, it's Croucher's. The same goes for Betty and Mosher Islands, and a whole raft of locations along the coast—just add *s* and you've got the local name. In telling the stories of the people who lived in these places, it makes the most sense to use these names, and this is what I've done.

1

The Lightkeepers

"Oh My God! Don't you get lonely out there? You must be a very solitary person!"

You're at a party, and someone has just learned that you're a lightkeeper. You can almost hear the mental gears moving. "Wow! He lives at a lighthouse! That's a crazy job! What makes this guy tick? He must be a real loner!" And the list goes on.

You could be surrounded by doctors, lawyers, nurses, architects—skilled professionals with demanding, complex and exciting jobs—but it doesn't matter. Everyone wants to know about the lightkeeper and his or her life. Lightkeeping was never rocket science, but it still has a mystique and allure that far outshines the reality (although sometimes the truth of lighthouse life was a bit stranger than fiction).

So you smile and say, well, it's really not unlike any other job. Fewer people around. More sea and sky. Time to think about life—in between weather reports, maintenance and the other myriad chores that crop up when you live on the edge of the sea.

There's more to the job than that, of course. It does take a certain mindset to be able to exist in physical isolation with minimal social contact. That is, assuming you're geared for urban living in the first place. If you're not, then it's not a difficult thing to be "stuck" on a lightstation, away from traffic and billboards and crowds.

But on an isolated lightstation, "living in each other's back pocket," as one keeper put it, *can* make it difficult to get along with your neighbours. A tantalizingly brief quotation from Coast Guard departmental correspondence in 1967 more than hints at friction between two lightkeepers:

Walter Mclaughlin spent thirty-five years tending lonely Gannet Rock. This may explain the look in his eyes.

> I got the impression from Mr. Campbell that his assistant keeps very irregular watch-keeping hours and that he was not altogether certain just what hours the assistant was on duty. Apparently

there has been very little communication between them since the shooting incident some time back.

Aside from armed conflicts, the real challenge can often be just getting along with yourself. After the busy summer maintenance schedule and the regular slate of weather observations, there's a fair bit of time for reflection and navel-gazing. I know I sometimes had too little work and too much time to think. But that was just a small drawback to being a lightkeeper at the end of the days of staffed lights in Nova Scotia.

Time to contemplate life and nature was not uppermost in the minds of the early keepers. Most were too busy trying to eke out a living on a paltry salary, while living in exposed, draughty buildings.

Until electricity and automation, lightkeeping was a labour-intensive affair, often breaking men and women with the demands of being on night-watch, hauling supplies, stoking fog whistle boilers, repairing broken-down engines, keeping livestock, and living with the knowledge that the sea could rip their work and lives apart at any given moment.

What kind of person would want to live this life? The popular image would be the loner, the misfit, or the man content to sip tea through the long evening watches while his steadfast light pierced the darkness of a stormy night.

He'd sport a thick beard, possibly a wooden leg, and he'd have been a sailor or a fisherman in his youth. He'd be a man whose clear blue eyes—while belying his great age—would hint at his vast knowledge about the weather, about nature and about God.

Okay, that's a pretty overblown stereotype, perpetuated by Hollywood, popular myth, and the tendency to romanticize the lightkeeping experience. In reality, lightkeeping attracted people who needed the work. If not well-paid, it was a steady job, providing a home for a family and a chance to make a decent life. Most nineteenth century lightkeepers had been seafarers of some sort, and knew what to expect when they moved out to tiny islands and isolated headlands.

Nova Scotia's (and Canada's) first lightkeeper was Jean Grenard *dit* Belair. Born in Poitiers, France in 1674, Grenard came to Louisbourg, Cape Breton after serving with French troops in Placentia, Newfoundland.

He didn't have any formal education, but Grenard had done well in the French marine service, eventually rising to the rank of sergeant. He was also a carpenter, and after retiring and losing his first wife, Grenard remarried—he had seven children to support—and in 1734, at the age of sixty, he became keeper of the great stone lighthouse in Louisbourg.

He lived within the walled fortress, walking along the shore or paddling the mile across the harbour to tend his light. After climbing the tower, Grenard had to light thirty-one wicks, all feeding from a bronze basin holding cod-liver oil. It was hard work and Grenard didn't make a lot of money—about the same as a fisherman.

But it was a job, and with a still-growing family, Grenard had no choice. In fact, he worked until he died in 1744, at the age of seventy.

As a French lightkeeper keeping a French light, Grenard may have been hired under and performed his duties according to the rules and regulations of his homeland's already well-established lighthouse service. But it wasn't until after Confederation that a comprehensive set of criteria for Canadian lightkeepers came about. In 1867, the newly formed Department of Marine and Fisheries took control of lighthouses in the Maritimes from the various colonial authorities. It was a time of rapid growth in the lighthouse business, with fifty-three lightstations in Nova Scotia alone.

Each light had a keeper who had to be made of the right stuff. The department looked for conscientious men of a sober and industrious nature. It wouldn't do to have a laggard and a layabout in this very responsible position. (Don't forget, lighthouses meant the difference between life and death for many mariners; as late as 1953, lightkeeper instructions emphasized the importance of "skilful and faithful performance of their important duties upon which greatly depends the security of life and property engaged in navigation.")

By 1875 the Department of Marine and Fisheries had published a slim volume with a big title: *Rules and Instructions for the Guidance of Lighthouse Keepers and of Engineers in Charge of Steam Fog Alarms in the Dominion of Canada.* The little book laid out the rules of lightkeeping, from instructions regarding the lighting of lamps, to medical directions for keepers—if you had piles, dropsy, paleness or small pox, to say nothing of worms, *this* was your guide to healthy living on Canada's lightstations.

By 1901, *Regulations for the Admission of Light-Keepers in to the Service of the Government of Canada* stated prospective keepers should be between nineteen and forty years of age, present certificates of marital status and health, and show the ability to operate a boat. They had to also be able to read, write, cipher, and be of good moral character. In addition, the department also preferred its keepers to be married men. After all, they were more stable and came with built-in free labour for the onerous tasks of lightkeeping on isolated stations.

It was tacitly expected—though not official policy—that families would provide unpaid labour, thus eliminating the need for assistant keepers. This remained the case at some stations almost to the very end; at some Nova Scotia lights in the 1980s, if an assistant keeper went on holiday, he was not replaced and the station reverted to one-man or -family operation.

For many years, lightkeeping appointments were political. If you voted the wrong way, your chances of a plum lightkeeping job were slim to nil. If you did vote the right way, and then the government changed power, you often lost your job.

The department also favoured war veterans for lighthouse jobs. Jerseyman Island lightkeeper Irving Latimer had served in the Canadian Army. He was wounded during World War One at the battle of Vimy Ridge and after convalescing in Halifax, he moved to Radville, Saskatchewan, where he tried his hand at "pioneer prairie farming," as his son Russ Latimer remembered.

"Apparently it was slim pickings," with more "mealtimes than meals," he said, so Irving and his young family returned to Nova Scotia. In 1930, the department appointed Irving as keeper of the Jerseyman Island light, near Arichat. He was, Russ remembered, "one of the few remaining World War One veterans to receive a federal government position."

By the 1950s, appointments were less political and more based on qualifications. In the '60s, the Canadian Coast Guard (formed in 1962) looked for men with all-round mechanical, electrical and carpentry experience, and a pragmatic view of life.

As Arnold Wing remembered of his years on the Westerns' light, in Ontario's Georgian Bay, "You weren't out there to just sit and think and read a book." With a steady stream of lake boats depending on the Westerns' light and horn, there was no time for romance and daydreaming.

But aside from clear and stern instructions about the utmost importance of vigilance and a strong moral backbone, the Canadian government took a hands-off attitude towards its keepers. It was one way of running a lighthouse service on a shoestring budget.

The system certainly didn't encourage breaks for keepers. Many didn't take holidays at all. It was hardly worth it when you'd have to pay your replacement out of your own pocket and still be responsible for the station. Don Gallagher told me that his father did not take one day

Chebucto Head keeper Edward Gallagher (left) could do a little fishing between watches, but did not take one holiday in his twenty-two years at the lighthouse.

off in the twenty-two years (1928–1950) he served at Chebucto Head, at the southern entrance to Halifax Harbour.

"That's the way the regulations went," Don said. "He could have had a day off and left his assistant in charge or he could have gone for a week on vacation and put somebody in his place with his assistant, but he had to assume full responsibility. So when you think about it, I don't think anybody would have gone on vacation because the other guy could have done whatever he felt like and a ship go ashore, the light not get lit, something like that—but my father was still responsible."

Combine the lack of holidays with a vigorous and relentless work schedule—painting, night and fog watches, repairs to the light mechanism and foghorn machinery—and you had a gruelling way of life that could get you down once in a while.

Late supplies just added insult to injury. Government tenders normally delivered supplies (everything from coal to broomsticks) once or twice a year. If you ran out of food or fuel in between, you just made do. In June 1945, an exasperated lightkeeper on Green Island, BC scrawled a sarcastic remark on the margin of his logbook: "No boat this month no groceries, Lightkeeper lives on fresh air."

Early salaries weren't much to write home about either. In the first decade of the twentieth century, a lightkeeper could hope to make about six hundred dollars a year. If he ran a steam foghorn, he might get a thousand dollars—but then he had to pay a man to help him run the horn.

On August 29, 1928, the Civil Service of Canada issued a "Position Vacant" poster, inviting residents of Shag Harbour, NS, to apply for the position of lightkeeper on nearby Bon Portage Island. The annual salary was pegged at $930.

Morrill Richardson applied for and got the job. He also bought most of the island. It was a rough go at times—trying to support a family on a slim salary and the proceeds of a small farming operation—and Evelyn Richardson later wrote that during the lean years she occasionally had to borrow from their kids' piggy banks to help make ends meet.

Still, it was during the Depression, and it was a steady job. As Marie (Palmer) Stevens remembers of her days at the Owl's Head lighthouse on Nova Scotia's eastern shore, "Nobody had anything, but we were always well fed and clothed and warm. It was really tough times."

Lightkeeper salaries slowly improved. By 1953, the keeper at Cape Sable was making between $2,970 and $3,420 per annum, depending on his years of service. But the keeper still had to pay an assistant out of his own pocket. In this case, Benjamin Smith hired his son Sid for $135 a month. As stated in the contract between father and son (drawn up by the Department of Transport), "The assistant agrees faithfully to carry out the duties assigned to him by the Lightkeeper while this contract is in force and understands he is the personal employee of the Lightkeeper and not an employee of the Government of Canada."

It was an archaic system—lighthouse authorities in the US, Britain and Europe had hired assistant keepers for years. It also allowed for some exploitation of assistants, who sometimes suffered at the hands of unscrupulous keepers. Finally, in 1960, the Canadian lighthouse service caught up with the rest of the world, hiring assistant keepers as full federal employees.

When I started on the lights in 1989, the base salary for a level six assistant keeper was $22,651. Not a get-rich scheme at first glance, but when you factored in free furnace fuel, free rent, and helicopter rides to the mainland, well, it wasn't such a bad deal.

Today, an assistant lightkeeper on one of the few remaining staffed lights in Canada can make up to $42,000 a year, and a principal earns in the $50,000 range. If you're someone who can stand a bit of isolation and get along with your neighbour in close quarters, it's a pretty good life.

Today's keeper is likely to be have been a banker or a railroad worker or a scientist, especially on the west coast, where people from all walks of life come to the lights. On the east coast, most keepers have fishing or lightkeeping backgrounds. Many of the remaining keepers in Newfoundland come from generations of lighthouse guardians.

The Cape's lit!

One characteristic possessed by almost every lightkeeper, right until the last days of staffed lights, was dedication. This was partly due to the traditional need for constant vigilance over finicky kerosene lamps and manually operated foghorns. But there was more to it than that. Most keepers and their families loved their jobs and their way of life. As a result, they put a great deal of effort and care into helping guide mariners to safety, and the job gave them a real feeling of purpose.

Morrill Richardson kept the Bon Portage light from 1929 to 1964.

That dedication took a number of forms, as Anne (Richardson) Wickens—whose parents, Morrill and Evelyn kept the Bon Portage light near Shag Harbour—recalled.

"There was a journal of some kind that told the lightkeepers the exact moment of sunrise and sunset," Anne told me. "At sunset you lit the light right then and there and at sunrise you put it out right then and there, which of course meant getting up at four o'clock in the morning on summer mornings and staying up till around ten on summer evenings.

"The only lighthouse around us who paid much attention to this was Cape Sable. Cape Sable was *always* lit right at the minute and always out right at the minute. And this was the sort of thing my father tried to do. I remember him coming in, tearing through the kitchen, leaving the doors open behind him, to dash up the stairs saying '*The Cape's lit!*' It was a dreadful dereliction of duty and a disgrace to the whole Richardson clan not to do your duty at the very moment it was supposed to be done!"

Dedication notwithstanding, some keepers had other ideas about when the light should be lit. With her eyes closed and a small smile on her face, Anne remembered that her great-grandfather Ephraim Larkin—

keeper of the light on nearby Stoddart Island from the late 1890s until 1937—did not hold much truck with the notion of lights-on at the very moment of sunset. "On one occasion Dad mentioned to the old gentleman—he was in his eighties then—that, you know, the light wasn't being lit *right* when the sun went down. But grandfather had been a sea captain in the days of sail, and he did everything by the tide. Nothing meant much to him as far as days and nights were concerned, only the tide. So he didn't see any reason at all why his little inshore light should be lit before the tide brought the little local fishing boats in off the fishing grounds. In those days, he had a fish business, a farm and sold fresh vegetables to any ships that called. Sometimes quite large vessels and often American yachts would come in to the anchorage just off from his light, but no, that didn't matter. If they couldn't find their way in the dark it didn't matter. It was the fishing boats he cared about. So my father—with his (I'm sure grandfather thought) persnickity-ness—didn't get very far with Great-Grandfather Larkin!"

Reg Smith: "I'm never gonna be on no space shuttle!"

I'M NEVER GONNA BE ON NO SPACE SHUTTLE!

Aside from dedication, what else made a good lightkeeper? In the early years, mechanical proficiency, boat handling, and strong moral character would take you a long way in the lightkeeping world (to say nothing of voting for the right political party). But there was more to the job than nuts and bolts (and patronage). There was the challenge of existence in a world far removed from society. The dynamic of a two-family or two-keeper society could be very complicated and occasionally dangerous. On a small, isolated island with limited social contact, limited duties and a seemingly infinite amount of time, you had to be at peace with yourself to be a good lightkeeper.

With a life of lighthouses under his belt—first as a keeper's son in the 1940s, then as his father's assistant, and finally as a principal keeper in the 1980s and '90s—Reg Smith told me the makings of a good lightkeeper were pretty simple, but not necessarily easy.

"The first thing, you have to be comfortable with yourself. Now, you often hear someone sayin' that well, he *feels* pretty important, but do you feel important because of the job you're doin', or is it just your general attitude that you're comfortable with yourself? I never figured I was too damn important because there's been thousands of other lightkeepers before me and some of 'em a hell of a lot better than I was or ever would have been. I think bein' a lightkeeper *before* I joined the army made me more realistic about what my capabilities would be. I knew I didn't have the education. As far as education goes, I think probably I might manage a grade six or an eight, but I might manage in life skills a grade twelve or college graduate.

"When I joined the army, I didn't know what I was gettin' into. But I found out after 16 weeks of basic training that I'm gonna be a private. I haven't got the education to expect much more than what a private would do in the engineers—lay mines, build Bailey bridges. When you get to be head keeper on a lightstation, unless you've got other qualifications, that's all you're ever gonna be. So you might as well content yourself with the fact that, 'I'm here, this is what I gotta do, the hell with the rest of the world!' It's no good for me to go to Machias Seal Island [in the Bay of Fundy] and set up there for twenty-eight days—'Jeez, I hope the next time the space shuttle goes off that I'm on it!'"

Reg smiled wryly. "Let's be realistic about it—I'm never gonna be on no space shuttle!"

HIS COOKING IS SLOWLY KILLING HIM

No matter how comfortable some lightkeepers were with their own capabilities and limits, some just couldn't cope with the character and foibles of others. Add a dash of isolation, a pinch of grudge, and a dollop of cabin fever, and you had the recipe for a miserable situation.

Out on Flint Island, off Cape Breton's east coast, one relief keeper didn't last long. Lightkeeper Brenton Hopkins came into the house one afternoon in the 1950s and found his new assistant sitting in a chair and holding a twelve-shot .22 pistol. Hopkins was a no-nonsense kind of man who did not suffer fools gladly. As his son Alfred remembers, the young assistant spun the chamber, and held the gun up to his head.

Click.

"Dad looked at him basically and said, 'Are you f—in' retarded? What's your problem?' The relief keeper said, 'Oh, nothing. I'm just playing roulette.' Dad said, 'Well, it's a g-d good thing you don't have any bullets in the gun!' The assistant stopped the thing and give it a spin like that and a bullet fell out. He *did* have a bullet in the gun!" Alf shook his head. "Well, he didn't last long! The old man called the office and said, 'Get him the Jesus off my island! We're here alone, he shoots himself, I wonder who will get blamed?'"

In the 1950s, one lightkeeper on the west coast seemed to have a particularly hard time of it (although none of his assistants played Russian roulette). Roy Cook went through a string of keepers, who by his account were variously hell-bent on tampering with his radios, losing his personal tools, and "chopping holes in the basement floor." Excerpts from the keeper's official correspondence with the marine agent (the lightkeepers' boss) read like a litany of dissatisfaction and frustration:

McCrae is bushed. His cooking is slowly killing him. Never complains of a toothache on rainy days. On good days when I expect a hand with something he sends over for aspirin and stays in bed. I explained that on an island, he would have to make an effort to be more congenial or he would find the island smaller and his disposition becoming contagious. It is not my intention to burden you with my problems, only to acquaint you with the situation. I could go on indefinitely.

And "go on" he did. A lengthy letter written in late 1960 started out in a positive tone, extolling the virtues of the latest assistant. He was a good and conscientious worker, "which is rare in most of them," and apparently both men had the same idea about when the foghorn should be started—an important task in the days when most small boats did not have radar.

But then things went wrong. During a Sunday dinner with Cook and his wife, the assistant stared at the two-hundred-watt lightbulb over the kitchen table, declaring it to be dim. Later, as the assistant chatted with the keeper and his wife, he asked who else was in the house. He'd seen the keeper stretch and thought that he was signalling to someone. Later, Cook went over to the assistant's house to see how he was making out. The house was cold, and when he asked why, the man said the furnace was "haywire." The furnace was fine, Cook wrote, but "while in the basement he wanted to know what the wires were for and [said] he would have to trace them. Later upstairs he said this is a government stakeout and they wanted to find out what he knew about the light. I told him the light was no secret. Anyone could buy a list of lights or a chart."

By this time, the keeper knew that, given his assistant's fragile mental state, he couldn't be trusted to keep a watch. Accordingly, the keeper decided to stay up through the night and wee hours of the morning, helping him trace the supposed trouble with the furnace wires.

"All during the night," Cook complained, "he could not convince himself that Tree Point and Holliday Island were light[house]s, but boats in trouble. After showing the chart to him twice between two and three in the morning he admitted that he was turned around and had thought he was looking towards Lucy Island." He concluded: "There is more along this line. We are sending a carton of his stuff ashore and a letter to his mother in hope she lets us know how he is."

One can only wonder what became of the assistant, and if he ever recovered from his confused mental state.

Finally, the principal keeper found one good man. After three years of dealing with screwdriver stealers, radio tamperers and sunny-day headaches, Cook had something good to say about his assistant. He wrote again to the Marine Agent.

Although I should hate the thought of losing Dodwell, I suggest he be seriously considered for promotion. He has evidently had carpentry, mechanical and some electrical experience. When asked to do a job, it is done willingly and efficiently. I asked his wife if she felt bushed or missed the bright lights. She laughed and said if the "bright lights" meant Prince Rupert, she preferred Green Island. I think they are well-suited for a career as lightkeepers.

I'LL NEVER BE ABLE TO DO THIS!

Jim Guptill, too, was well-suited for a career as a lightkeeper. Around the time that Green Island's head keeper was reluctantly recommending his assistant for promotion, Jim was a fifteen-year-old heading with his family to Country Island, on Nova Scotia's eastern shore. His father, Keith Guptill, had just accepted the head keeper's position on the island,

Jim Guptill's best efforts as a lightkeeper were "established by routine."

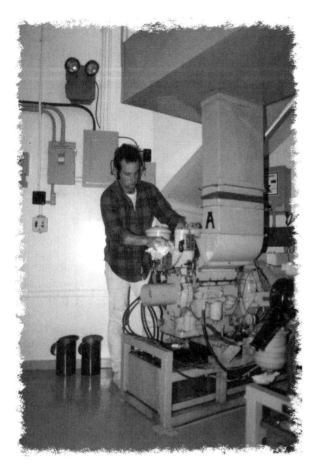

Checking the generators: a regular lighthouse duty.

much to Jim's chagrin—he had recently discovered girls—and all of a sudden it was time to move from downtown Canso to a scrubby spruce-covered island nearly five kilometres from shore.

But Jim took to lighthouse life like a duck to water, eventually becoming his father's assistant, and then moving off the island to keep lights on Gull Rock and the Salvages. He knew the routine. He also knew about the relationships between the lightkeeping families and respecting the privacy of your lightkeeping neighbours living just a few feet away—for instance, how one keeper getting ready for a night shift might want to catch a few winks in the early evening, "even if you want[ed] to be hauling gravel rocks with the tractor, by his bedroom window!"

So, there were compromises to be made. But by and large, life went by fairly smoothly. By 1974 Jim was married and had a young family. He decided to leave Country Island and take a rotational station, so that his children could attend school on the mainland. But as he stood on the water's edge at Gull Rock—a tiny strip of reef off Lockeport on the South Shore, with a squat lighthouse barnacled onto the ledge—Jim wasn't so sure about his new digs.

"I'll never be able to do this!" he told me thirty years later. "That was my thought with the boat alongside of us, the bow of it just touching on the skidway. Beautiful day. But I could picture what it would be like when it was rough and miserable and I really felt at that moment that I couldn't do it. I didn't want to be away from my family. I was twenty-nine years old in 1974, with a young wife, a young family and here I am cast away in the middle of this island. I knew exactly how

Robinson Crusoe felt! It was a devastating experience. The awful part of it was that I hadn't considered that part of it. I knew that I was looking after my family. I knew that I had made arrangements for my children's education. I knew all of that stuff, but nevertheless, here I am now standing at the water's edge on Gull Rock in the middle of August 1974 and I hadn't thought about Jim!"

The young keeper had some help settling in, though. Veteran keepers John Gwynn and Earl Flemming knew all about surviving for a month at a time in a twenty-six-foot-square house. Still, Jim had a

Spartan accommodations at the Salvages for keepers on 28-day shifts.

devil of a time trying to get into a daily work plan. "Our best effort is established by routine," he told me. "I had had a wonderful routine on Country Island. The whole thing had progressed very well there, and now suddenly here I am with no outside activity at all. Thankfully, the first month that I was there the house needed painting. So every daylight hour we used in painting. I was at that time timid of heights, so it was a slow, laborious process, but it saved my sanity."

But what about the issue of getting along with another lightkeeper not necessarily of your own choosing? For Jim, the question was, "What are you going to do for this twenty-eight days? That's a lot of hours, and you're stranded there with one man whether you like him or whether you don't! Ninety per

cent of the time you were alone because the other guy was sleeping, getting ready to go on for his shift. We stood twelve on and twelve off for twenty-eight days. My day for the day shift would start off at seven in the morning, have a half-hour yarn with the guy that was up all night, and he'd go away and you'd make your breakfast."

Then Jim would begin his work day, checking the generators, cleaning, painting and keeping a radio schedule with Halifax Coast Guard Radio. When it came time to launch the station boat, paint the buildings or do anything more complex, the two keepers worked together. But for the most part, many of the jobs could be completed by one person.

In England, isolated "rock" stations traditionally had three keepers. This created a different social situation than on the Canadian two-man stations. Arthur Lane spent a few years as assistant keeper on the famous Eddystone light, off Plymouth. In his book, *It Was Fun While It Lasted*, he reflected on the dynamics of the three-man system, which he described as "unparalleled" anywhere in society.

> Even in a three-man prison the cell door is unlocked from time to time to allow association with other prisoners. To be confined in a lighthouse was not to be confined in a cell, true; but in the level of its social insularity I cannot think of a rival.

If it was true, as Lane wrote, that "what a man had to offer was in his head," then "it was a miracle if two men could still have something interesting to say to each other at the change of watch." How could you remain sane, cooped up with another person for weeks on end? Having three keepers instead of two helped, according to Lane.

> The interdependence of three men had the effect of discouraging extremes of behaviour. When clashes occurred they tended to be across the generations, where there could be a forty-year age gap between a Principal Keeper and a young Assistant. However, there were more favourable factors working for harmony than outsiders might think.

Those factors included a watch system that left one man alone throughout the evening and morning hours. For the rest of the day, two keepers were up and about, but one would likely be doing something in the kitchen and the other fishing, or keeping up with correspondence. And then there would be a breath of fresh air, as one keeper or two would go on shore leave, to be replaced by his or their relief. The Trinity House (English lighthouse authority) system stipulated a "more radical refreshment" every three years, when one keeper would be posted to another lighthouse. As Lane noted, three keepers on a tower rock formed "a self sustaining society with curiously effective checks and balances."

Jim Guptill at the Salvages: "It was best if you didn't get too close to the person you were there with."

Back in Canada, there was a decided lack of those checks and balances. With just two keepers on a station, and no long-term plan that saw keepers moving from station to station, things could get pretty hairy if you didn't get along with your shift partner. I worked with one keeper who, after a while, shut himself in his room to roll cigarettes and watch television. He would emerge at regular intervals to prepare weather observations, transmit them, and then disappear into his room again. In no way was he derelict in his lighthouse duties; he just didn't want to talk to me. I'm not sure why. Some days we'd share no more than a dozen words between us. It was a tough situation to be in when you were stuck in one spot for a month, with nowhere to run.

Jim Guptill told me his time on Gull Rock worked out well. He got along with his fellow keepers, they devised a routine that kept the station in good shape, and Jim was left to spend his off-time reading, exercising, keeping in touch with penpals, and baking. With a transfer to the Salvages—a string of reefs off Nova Scotia's South Shore—the situation changed a little. When I interviewed Jim, I wanted to get to the heart of the matter about interpersonal relationships on the lights: the grit, the drama and the conflict. Jim was very diplomatic when I asked, "How was the personnel situation there?"

"Ahh…sometimes good, sometimes not," he said, carefully. "From my experience, it was best if you didn't become too close to the person that you were there with, because you would tend to play on their nerves and annoy them if you did that. It was best to set up your own pastime, your own day-to-day routine, and then fit each other into it, rather than depending upon each other to be that routine. I found that with most people, watching the evening news was sort of a get-together time. But I was on with people that found drinking a nice habit and I didn't, because if you're doing twenty-eight twelve-hour shifts in a row, there's not a lot of time to get drunk. During my second winter at Salvages I had a chap that I would find in a drunken stupor a time or two when I arrived to go on shift. And excuse me, but when it's blowin' forty knots out of the west and cold and the old furnace in the basement is spewing out fire and this guy's lying there drunk—well, I didn't put up with it very long."

But Jim told me that for the most part, keepers got along quite well.

"Most people are excellent. And they're more excellent under isolation, by the way. You develop a sort of a dependence upon each other when you're in those circumstances. It's a physical dependence for one thing, because if you hurt yourself, that's the only other person in your life at that moment that can help out. Number one. Number two is that people like people as a rule. If all else is equal, folks like folks. So that is in your favour. And most of the time—99.9 per cent of the time—this interchange between the two men there was a marvellous experience."

GOOD FOR COUGHS, COLDS, ITCHY HOLES…

People are people, and lightkeeping, more often than not, was largely defined by the characters who kept the light. It may be that the way of life attracted a certain type of person. It may also hold true that the

Peter Coletti and a friend, on Gannet Rock.

job helped turn people into "characters." Living away from civilization would sometimes bring out little character foibles that could be amusing, annoying, or just plain interesting.

When I look back at my own nine years on the lights—and more than thirty years of visiting lighthouses—I can see and hear a collage of characters as plainly as if they were all in the same room with me now. I remember my friend Peter Coletti, who had come to work on Gannet Rock after spending a couple of decades on Great Lakes lights. Peter had (and still has) an insatiable interest in all things mechanical, and the lighthouse kitchen was often littered with parts of cameras, guns (with special permission from the Coast Guard, as Gannet was a "firearms free" zone) and other paraphernalia. Peter was one of those keepers who liked to decorate day-to-day life with jokes and stories (mostly unprintable). He had a parrot who came out for one month-long shift and I still enjoy watching the video I made of Peter filing the bird's beak and claws—much to the delight of the parrot—with a large

A couple of characters ham it up to help pass a long winter's night on Gannet Rock in the early 1990s.

metal file. He also decorated household items, such as the bottle of Spray Nine cleaner above the kitchen sink, which, aside from the usual warnings, read "Good for coughs, colds, itchy holes, and pimples on the pididdlehopper."

I can see one of the keepers on Machias Seal Island, wearing a pair of disposable white coveralls with the crotch ripped out and the words "Puffin Surgeon" scrawled across the back in magic marker. We're sitting on the back porch of the keepers house, with a few thousand terns, puffins, and razorbill auks creating a massive, discordant din in the background. We're taking a break from mowing the lawn, which during the summer involved wearing hard hats with top-mounted flags to ward off dive-bombing arctic terns. The "Puffin Surgeon" takes a last draw on his cigarette and we get back to work.

I can see dinnertime on Gannet Rock with another keeper—hamburgers fried beyond recognition and potatoes boiled beyond belief. Then a swig of Pepsi and "Ah, that's good! It cuts the grease!"

I can see Huck Norwood's annotated copy of the lightkeeper's manual, complete with instructions to "be sure to untie boat if you want to leave wharf," and a warning posted to keep the paint cupboard locked because of a number of recent "paint thefts." All this on a rock nine miles out to sea with a population of two.

Some keepers had other foibles. One west coast guardian insisted that his assistant and the assistant's wife wave at every ferry boat that passed the station. This meant dropping what you were doing, running to the landing, and dutifully waving to the tourists lining the decks of the vessel. One day, the assistant and his wife noticed that the response from the ferry was more fervent than usual, with much cheering and blowing of horns. The assistant looked over to his wife, and his jaw dropped, after seeing that her tube top had inadvertently let go from its moorings and was now resting somewhat lower than it would normally be. For months afterwards officers on the ferry made many requests for the "nice lady" to wave at them again!

It's likely that outsiders, even those who worked on the water, often wondered what made lightkeepers tick. When the same couple did a relief stint on a rotational "rock" station, they liked to take an evening stroll on the helicopter pad. Dressed in lumberjack shirts, the pair presented an intriguing sight to a passing fisherman, who remarked it was "about time those fellas got off that rock!"

Some couldn't wait to get away from the job and the isolation. When I first went to Gannet Rock I made a video for the other keeper there, who wanted to pass it along to friends ashore. He'd made no secret of his disillusionment with lighthouse life—he'd been at it for years and still wasn't full-time, and he was pissed off at a Coast Guard that wouldn't commit to someone who'd been at the job for more than five years. On the day we shot our "Day in the Life" video, he made up a cardboard sign with "Boulevard of Broken Dreams" inked on it, attaching it to the side of the concrete house. I panned from the sign to the keeper, leaning on the railing above the seawall, pensively drawing on a cigarette while staring out to sea.

Within a year he'd left Gannet Rock and lightkeeping for good.

Today there are just a few dozen lightkeepers in Canada, compared to more than eight hundred at the turn of the last century. Their job and way of life has changed much over the years, but for the most part, the basic outlook and dedication remain, along with the eccentricities.

But no shooting incidents lately, as far I know.

2

The
Nuts and Bolts
OF LIGHTKEEPING

FROM THE VERY BEGINNING, THE RAISON D'ETRE OF the lightkeeper was to keep the light burning. Egypt's Pharos at Alexandria—built around 280 BC—kept its attendants engaged in a nightly struggle with an open wood fire. Working in wind and rain at the top of the 130-metre structure, they were often exasperated by their puny efforts against the elements.

The Romans built a series of lights across their burgeoning empire—these too had keepers who fed sticks into braziers through the long nights. After 400 AD, a period of darkness fell upon the empire's coasts, as Rome slowly collapsed. Not until after 1600 did European authorities begin to vigorously pursue lighthouse-building programs.

By the late seventeenth century, many European lighthouses burned coal instead of wood, producing a more consistent, if not much brighter, flame. The eighteenth century was marked by what lighthouse historian D. Alan Stevenson called "remarkable improvements" in aids to navigation, with the development of fish- and whale-oil lights intensified by metal or glass reflectors. These advances made lights brighter than they'd ever been. Still, keepers had to contend with congealed fuel, smoky lamps and drafty towers. The crude reflector systems made their lights more powerful than a plain open flame, but still required constant vigilance, constant repairs, and constant cleaning.

It wasn't until 1822 that lighthouse technology really took off, with the development of the Fresnel lens. French physicist Augustin Fresnel joined the French lighthouse service in 1813, throwing his efforts into solving the "vexing" problem of light diffusion. By 1822, Fresnel had designed a lens system that used a central magnifying bullseye surrounded by concentric prisms to gather and direct light into a concentrated beam. Fresnel's invention

The centre of a lightkeeper's life—the lens. This one guided ships past Gannet Rock from 1904 to 1967.

The lightkeeper on top of the lantern gives scale to the massive first-order lens at Langara Point in Haida Gwaii, BC. It's the only type of its kind still in use in Canada.

A seventh-order Fresnel lens, used commonly around Nova Scotia in small harbour and island lights.

revolutionized lighting systems in lighthouses around the world. His lenses came to be classed in seven main orders, from the first to the sixth (with a three-and-a-half-order lens thrown into the mix). There was also the massive hyper-radial lens, a five-and-a-half-tonne Goliath standing more than six metres (twenty feet) high. On the other end of the scale, lighthouse manufacturers Chance Brothers also made a mouse of a lens—a seventh-order—standing just under twenty-nine centimetres (11 and 1/8 inches) high, but still with exquisite hand-polished lenses and a brass frame.

The powerful hyper-radial and first- and second-order lenses crowned landfall lights like that at Cape Race Newfoundland, where a gleam of light was both a greeting and a reassurance to transatlantic ships that they had made it safely across the pond. The little lenses—fifth-, sixth- and seventh-orders—performed the same task on a smaller scale, guiding modest fishing schooners and coastal traffic into little harbours all around the Maritimes.

The next leap forward in lighthouse illumination came from Nova Scotia, with Abraham Gesner's development of coal oil, or kerosene. The geologist was born near Cornwallis, in the Annapolis Valley, in 1797. After moving to Saint John, he discovered veins of coal, which he used in distillation experiments. Gesner later moved to the United States, where he developed and patented a process for the manufacture of kerosene. By 1853 he had perfected the lamp oil that was to become the standard lighting fuel for homes and lighthouses around the world. Kerosene produced a clean, powerful light. With the development of compressed air/kerosene systems, called IOV (incandescent oil vapour) burners, the stage was set for an efficient lighthouse lighting system.

In the meantime, there was the question of what do when it was too foggy for the light to be seen. Some lighthouse authorities used cannons to sound warnings in thick weather. Later, bells came into vogue. But the fog warning system found a new standard thanks to Robert Foulis, a civil engineer born in Glasgow, Scotland. Foulis moved to Saint John, New Brunswick, where he developed and patented a steam fog whistle. He presented his design to the province's lighthouse commissioners in

1853, but it wasn't until seven years later that his invention was installed on Partridge Island in Saint John Harbour. Foulis was later recognized as the inventor of the world's first steam-powered fog whistle. Later, lighthouse authorities and manufacturers developed various horns, sirens, and trumpets, culminating in the mighty air-powered diaphone, with its famous deep "blast and grunt" signal.

All this equipment—scintillating lenses and resonating foghorns—needed a keeper's tender care. The seemingly simple act of presenting a guiding light and horn for mariners was in fact the result of a number of complex procedures. In a world where many mechanical functions are now automatic, it is difficult to conceive of the amount of work that went into operating a lightstation. From winding the weights that ran a

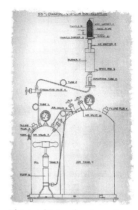

The workings of an incandescent oil vapour burner, from a 1912 Marine and Fisheries manual.

Men did not always rule their machines—fog alarm engines gave many lightkeepers untold amounts of grief.

light's clockwork rotating mechanism, to cleaning out vapour burners, to polishing brass and gently cleaning lenses with a chamois, the work was relentless.

Fog whistles and horns added another dimension of fun tasks—imagine crawling into a steam whistle's fire box to clean out the clinkers, or spending hours replacing tubes in massive boilers. When the coal ran out, keepers had to cut and split wood to feed the boiler's ravenous maw. The change to diesel-powered compressors lessened the work load a bit, but then there was another set of issues to deal with: worn valves, broken fuel lines, frayed belts, and anything else that can and will go wrong with an internal combustion engine.

One west coast keeper went so far as to name his foghorn engine. "Lizzie" gave him two decades of grief, behaving like a cranky "invalid despite all his rehabilitation efforts, and the hours he spent tarting up her brasswork." After twenty years of replacing gaskets, grinding valves, cleaning manifolds, and cleaning up the oil spewed by "Lizzie,"

Incandescent oil vapour lights needed air and kerosene to operate. The keeper used the bicycle-type pump in the middle to pressurize the system.

the keeper finally got a break, when he transferred to another station. It was a short-lived reprieve—he soon learned that the engines at the new station were in worse shape than his old nemesis!

Throughout the late nineteenth century and for six decades into the twentieth, lightkeeping remained very much a hands-on affair. It was only when electricity relieved keepers of the long night watch over a roaring kerosene light and a bellowing foghorn that the job changed in any great way. Electricity also brought fridges, freezers, television and other conveniences. But it was the beginning of the end. Soon, electrical devices would take away the very tasks that were once vital to the operation of a lightstation.

SHE WOULD TAKE OFF!

At the age of twelve, Reg Smith was literally at the top of his profession—101 feet in the air. To be entirely accurate, it was his father's job, but young Reg was given light-up responsibilities at Cape Sable very early on. Near sunset he would climb the massive concrete tower to begin the evening ritual. It was a dangerous process.

"The person that turned the light off in the morning," Reg told me, "it was his job to pump the fuel up to the tank and fill the tank with the kerosene for the next night. There was one tank for kerosene and one for air. You always shut the air tank off when you put the light out, and you would pump the pressure back up on the tank for the guy that was gonna light it." When it came time to light up, "the most dangerous part was heatin' the burner, 'cause you used wood alcohol to heat the burner up. If you didn't get the burner hot enough, well then you had a big flame goin', so you had raw kerosene goin' through the system and it would be just like a blow torch.

"At the bottom of the burner there was a little tray with a trough. You filled that with wood alcohol and lit it. In the summertime one spoonful was sufficient to warm your tube enough to light the vapourized kerosene. In the wintertime, you might have to give it two shots. If it was real cold, you always made sure you put your next spoonful of alcohol in while it was still burnin', because if you poured the wood alcohol in on the hot burner, you'd have an explosion. Then you had a little pricker. There's a very small hole at the top of the burner tube and you used this pricker to clean that hole out. Then you'd turn the air on and then just light a match and hold it near the mantle, and she would take off—*if* everything worked right!"

The system was pretty reliable. But what happened when there was a malfunction? Quite simply, it was a lightkeeper's nightmare, as Reg's cousin, Sid Smith, can attest to. "You had kerosene under pressure coming into this vapourizing tube and it came out of the top of the tube through a little pin hole," he told me. "That was just vapour. Some of that was brought back down and through little burners on the side,

Sid Smith showing the operation of a 55mm incandescent oil vapour burner from the Cape Sable lighthouse. Raw kerosene through the burner could cause flare-ups, leaving keepers with a massive clean-up in the lantern.

Keepers had to be up every two to four hours to wind the clockwork mechanism that rotated their lens.

Several hundred kilograms of weights descended from a lighthouse clockwork mechanism. If the weights happened to run though your house, you could expect some damage if they ever "let go."

and these kept the tube hot so the next batch of kerosene coming along would also get hot and vapourize. It was very much like a Coleman lantern, only much bigger.

"But if those pilot lights that kept the tube hot went out, then your kerosene came out as raw kerosene instead of vapour. It burned, and what a mess! How many times have I looked up there and said, 'Oh, should I go up there and put it out or should I just set here and cry?' If you happened to catch this thing before it had been doing this for very long, why, it might not be too bad. It might only be a day to clean it up! But if it started acting up just after you'd checked on the thing and it had been ten minutes in the process of burning raw kerosene, all the Fresnel lens, the iron work up overhead even, the window frames, even the windows themselves would have about an eighth of an inch of a black grease on them. All the glasswork and those prisms—all the soot seemed to be on the inside somewhere you couldn't get at. It wasn't something you could take down and wash!"

The job wasn't finished after hours or days of cleaning. Then came the re-painting. Sid and his father would have to coat everything in aluminum paint first, and then apply the white. As Sid told me, the whole procedure was "an awful thing." In December 1960, the one piece of automation he liked put an end to the flaring kerosene problem—an electric lightbulb in the lens.

As well as watching for flaring in those pre-electricity days, the keeper had to be up through the night to make sure the light was rotating. Cape Sable lasted four hours on a winding. Reg Smith described the process to me.

"The man on watch in the mornin' wound the weights back up. Then there was a set of bars you could put across the hole that the weights would come down and set on, and that's where they'd be at night. So in the evenin' when you went up to light you'd just have to wind a few cranks on the spindle, lift the weights off the bars and then pull the bars out and the weight would start the light turnin'. I always used to push it for good luck, so the damn thing wouldn't stop sometime through the night!"

Some keepers used electrical contacts to tell them when their weights needed winding. Others placed a mirror near a window in their home where they could observe the rotating beam of light, and still sit or stretch out on a daybed for a catnap. One trusting keeper reportedly went so far as to place a board on his chest and then nap directly below the weights as they descended though his lighthouse. The pressure of the weights would awaken him to his duty.

It sounds like a pretty risky method. Some clockwork systems used 160 kilograms (350 pounds) or more of weights to rotate a light, and the cables they were placed on sometimes parted. If the weights were to fall, it would be fatal for the luckless man sleeping beneath and dangerous too, for anyone else nearby.

In the case of the lighthouse at Chebucto Head, keeper Edward Gallagher and his family lived directly underneath the lantern and clockwork mechanism. Edward's son Don told me the cables for the weights ran down through the house, leading to an interesting incident one windy night.

"There was this ungodly crash. Either a pulley came out or else one of the pins in one of the pulleys wore through over the years and the cable broke. Down went the weights, down the shaft. It was just after it was wound up so the weights fell the whole height of the house. She came all the way down and went through the hardwood floor in a little bedroom that was off the living room. It went right through there and ended up in the cistern."

He shook his head. "Oh my Lord! It sounded like they turned the six-inch guns on us from down at the Cape! What a racket! It was unreal. It reverberated through the whole house. We were all home at the time, but weren't in any danger because it went down this shaft that was built in the corner of the house. But if a fella had been in a bed alongside of it he mighta got moved around a couple of feet! The floor had all smashed to heck."

Adventures with flaring kerosene and plummeting weights aside, there was still work to do at sunrise. In the days before the Coast Guard decreed that all lights were to be left turning twenty-four hours a day, you shut your light down at dawn. According to the 1953 edition of *Rules and Instructions For Lightkeepers and Fog Alarm Engineers and Rules*

Cleaning the lens.

Governing Buoys and Beacons, "Lamps and apparatus are to be cleaned daily as hereinafter described."

28. The glass prisms and lenses of a dioptric apparatus are to be cleaned every day when in use, being first freed from dust by using a slightly damp cloth, and then rubbed perfectly clean and dry with a soft cheese cloth.

29. If the glass becomes greasy, it should first be washed with a clean cloth steeped in methylated spirits then carefully dried with a soft cloth free from all dust or grit, and finally rubbed with a fine flannelette or cheese-cloth.

It was also important, the instructions stated, to test the level of the lens from time to time as it would be "fatal" to the efficiency of the light if the apparatus was out of plumb or the lamp out of focus. The rules also decreed that the blinds be put down and lenses be covered during the daylight hours. This served a more important purpose than just keeping dust off the lens. The bullseyes in the centre of each lens panel were capable of magnifying the sun and starting fires, inside the lantern or even on the ground below.

Think back to your childhood, when you or a friend scorched a poor caterpillar with a magnifying glass on a sunny day. In my early thirties, while lightkeeping in British Columbia, I inadvertently found myself on the other side of the glass. I had shut down the massive first-order lens at Langara Point in Haida Gwaii (also known as the Queen Charlotte Islands) to clean the prisms. As I stood in the middle of the

1 Lighting the two wicks in the duplex lamp inside a seventh-order lens.

2 With the wicks turned low, the keeper would put the chimney on the lamp.

3 After the chimney had warmed up, the keeper could turn the wicks up for a brighter light.

4 After lighting up, the keeper was to remain in the lantern for thirty minutes, "attending to the flame of the lamps."

glittering three-metre-high lens, Windex and soft cloth in hand, I felt
a rather curious and extremely painful burning sensation on my left
shoulder. Much like the unfortunate caterpillars in my distant past, I
was experiencing the concentrated effects of sunlight, through the lens'
huge bullseye.

I moved out of the way before my shirt caught fire.

It Gave an Excellent Light

Keepers at smaller harbour and island lights around the Maritimes
followed similar routines to their colleagues at larger landfall stations,
albeit on a reduced scale. With just a small fixed (instead of flashing)
light and no foghorn to worry about, it was primarily a case of lighting
the light at sunset and putting it out in the morning.

Ivan Kent's grandfather, father and mother kept the French Point
light near Musquodoboit Harbour, starting in 1903. Ivan still lives next
to the lighthouse in the family homestead. Since 1951, the light has
come on by itself each night, but when Ivan was a boy, it still needed the
human touch.

"It was a big brass lamp, held about a gallon or so kerosene, with
a double wick and a normal lamp shade," Ivan told me. "'Course, that
all had to be cleaned every night and the lamp filled and the wicks
trimmed. You let it burn till you got a good blaze on each wick without
any smoke. Then there was a red sector went down over. The lamp had
two hooks and the prism [lens] was sittin' up on a bench quite high, so
you took these hooks and lifted the lamp up and then lowered it inside
the prism. It was visible for about fourteen miles to sea. It gave an excellent light."

Growing up on Croucher's Island in Saint Margaret's Bay,
Geraldine (Boutilier) Stevens remembered it was an important task to
keep the lantern and lens clean. Every Sunday her father, Wentworth
Boutilier, would bring the brass kerosene lamp down to the kitchen to
clean it. The procedure was a "big thing" for Geraldine and her sisters. "We kids used to just sit there and watch him! We saw Dad doing

something that we kind of thought maybe a woman would do—clean the lamp, for one thing," Geraldine remembered. "Oh, he used to make it so you could see your face in it!"

FOGHORNS

Along with the lens and its associated lamps, burners, gears and weights, the foghorn was the other big time-consumer for keepers. On some stations, from the early twentieth century until the late 1950s, the hand-operated horn kept lightkeepers and family members alert for signals from small boats looking for guidance. At bigger stations with "automatic," horns, it was crucial to keep a fog watch. Each station had a set of markers it would use to judge the time when the horn should be fired up. At Cape Sable, Sid Smith and his father would start up the diaphone when they lost sight of a buoy four miles south west of the light.

"Everything was all set up to go before you left the engine room after you shut it off the last time," Sid recalled. "You pulled on the air brake and got the engine started, then when it got up to speed, you threw the compressor into gear. When your air pressure got up to thirty pounds, you turned on your timing devices, which is a rig that has these little dogs on it. You had pulleys on the engine and on the timing device, the proper size that would make the timing device dogs come around every twenty seconds. This gave you a three-second blast and seventeen seconds [of] silence. All stations have their own characteristic, so if your charts says Cape Sable has seventeen seconds [of] silence and a three-second blast, well that's what it had to be. Those old Vivians [diesel engines], you could set the speed on them and so we always had a stop watch and you would set them so they were blowin' the proper blast and maintaining the proper air pressure at all times."

Jim Guptill remembered that were was "a lot of adjusting to do," so that everything ran just the way it was supposed to. "These engines, sometimes, when they were running cold, wouldn't compress as much air as they would when you arrived at a good running temperature for them. So you had to keep a constant eye on the machinery as it powered these horns. In the wintertime, if your engine room was warm and your wind was southwest and your fog was in, the wind would suddenly come to the northwest and you'd get snow squalls. Your engine room would cool down and your air pressure would go for a dump. You were always in and out of the engine room all the time. These old air horns could make a really dreadful sound when the air pressure was off somewhat. It was more like a bleat at the end of it when the air pressure was up, or a bad grunt when it was down!"

ALL THERE WAS, WAS BLOOD AND FEATHERS!

Along with the bleating and grunting and the clamour of machinery, the engine room was a dangerous place to work. Back in the '30s and '40s, stations with the big diaphone foghorns used massive Fairbanks Morse single-cylinder engines. Puffing and sweating and growling in their engine room lairs, these monsters had large, spoked flywheels. To start the engine, it was a matter of standing on those spokes to get the flywheel moving and then engaging the compression, all the while making damn sure your legs weren't going to become part of the machinery. As a young teenager, Reg Smith was too light to do the job alone at Cape Sable, so it was a mother-and-son team that got the engine going.

There was danger outside the engine room as well. Out on Flint Island, off Cape Breton's Port Morien, you took your life in your hands when it was time to start the winch in the boathouse. Although the old one-lunger was only rated at five horsepower, it could, as lightkeeper's son Alf Hopkins remembered, "haul hell out by the roots. It had a big flywheel on it, but you could get your hands on to it. It looked like a wheel for a cart, but big and heavy. You would take that and rock it back and forth and it would start either way, which was the dangerous part. You got it whichever way you wanted, till it just hit that compression point and then you'd give it to it on the other way and it would go past the compression point—and bump-bump-bump-bump it would start."

Flywheeled monsters in their "engine room lair," Seal Island, c.1910.

Alf's father, Brenton Hopkins, had a knack with the cantankerous beast. But newcomers often got a shock when they tried to start the engine and it decided to kick back. Alf recalled that "For one of the poor guys trying to learn how to do it, the engine threw him half the length of the boathouse. It's a wonder it hadn't a' damn killed him!"

Once they were operating, keepers still had to be wary of these chuffing beasts. In his book about the lights of British Columbia's north coast, Don Graham recounts how a winch engine almost cost a light-keeper's wife her life.

Tom and Sophie Moran lived on Triple Island, a tiny rock about forty-eight kilometres (thirty miles) west of Prince Rupert. In late 1929 they were preparing to haul a load of wood up to the station. As Sophie stood at the controls "…the flywheel snatched and grabbed the hem of her dress, wrenching her off her feet. Sophie tore away at the seam and grabbed, then tried to crawl away, fingernails clawing the floor. It was a tug-of-war she could never hope to win, just one woman against all that thundering horsepower. Each turn of the flywheel drew her closer to the machine's deadly metal embrace. Shrieking in fear, she braced her arms against the hot block, then was spun around, dragged backwards up against the flywheel, and became a human spoke."

Wondering at the delay from above, Tom finally heard his wife's screams over the roar of the engine and scrambled for the winch house. Cutting her free from "the iron molars of the machinery, dripping grease and gore," he nursed her as well as he could without medical supplies. The government tender picked Sophie up a week later and took her to hospital. She recovered and returned to Triple Island. (Because she was her husband's employee, the Canadian government denied

"A potentially deadly obstacle course." The engine room at Cape Sable in the 1950s. Note the belts between the machinery.

Sophie any compensation for her horrific injuries.)

Back at Nova Scotia's Cape Sable, a room full of engines meant it didn't hurt to have light feet. Large leather belts ran off the flywheels, to power water pumps and timing devices. This machinery, linked by vibrating, flapping leather bands, turned the engine room into a potentially deadly obstacle course. It didn't seem to phase some of the keepers, as Sid Smith remembered.

"I've seen Dad and my Uncle Alfie crawl through the belts while the engines were running but I wouldn't crawl through them! 'Course, we were only kids. We weren't allowed to, but I've seen them go through. I imagine if they were both living today they could say that wasn't being very smart!

"I gotta tell you a little story," he added. "My Uncle Alfie just loved going gunning. One day the wind was to the sou'west and he was out by the engine room and these sea ducks were comin' down from the nor'west and going right by the point. Uncle Alfie had this old single-barrel shotgun. I know the thing killed more on the back end than it did on the front because he was alway skinned up around the nose from shootin' that old shotgun! Anyway, he shot this sea duck. The thing just scaled down and went right in through the engine room window. It went right under those belts and went around on the flywheels and, well! Us kids went runnin' to see what happened to that duck! All there was, was blood and feathers. You wouldn't believe the mess! So that's what happened when you tried to get in between the belts!"

Sid Smith working on a fog signal engine at Cape Sable in the 1950s.

Aside from the dangers to humans and stray ducks, Sid felt at home in the engine room, the heart of the Cape Sable lightstation. "I always enjoyed the engine room for some reason and once we got generators in it, why, it was just that much nicer. You had fog alarm engines and generators going. It took a lot of fuel to keep everything topped up. We had an office out there where you could set back and put your feet up on the desk and right out the big window in front of the office you could watch the engines workin'." He smiled. "The engine room was a nice place for me."

THEY'D JUST SHOOT HALFWAY OUT OF THE WATER AND ROLL OVER ON ONE SIDE

It took a lot of gear to run a lightstation—kerosene, diesel, paint, tools, mantles for the light, foghorn parts, mops, brooms. You name it, you

Government supply ship *Edward Cornwallis* at Beaver Harbour Head, NS, in 1955.

needed it. Cleaning supplies for the light, and all manner of provisions came once or twice a year to all lights. The Department of Marine and Fisheries had a long line of supply ships that spent their working lives ducking into bays, harbours and isolated land-based lighthouses to deliver everything from pianos to broomsticks.

For little stations like Croucher's Island, there'd be oil for the light, some coal for the keeper, wicks, logbooks, mops, soap and anything else needed to run a small light. Unloading the provisions usually took a few hours, and during that time the district inspector would come to look the light over and talk with the keepers about any problems or issues. At bigger stations, such as Chebucto Head at the entrance to Halifax Harbour, a visit from the government tender was a big production, involving much moving of supplies from ship to workboat to shore. Today you can drive right to the lighthouse, but back in the 1930s and '40s, the only highway to Chebucto Head was wide and watery.

Landing supplies at the base of a hundred-foot granite cliff amidst roiling seas was always tricky and never dull, as Don Gallagher remembered with wide eyes and plenty of arm waving.

"There were two supply boats. There was one called the *Lady Laurier* and there was another one used to come once in a blue moon was called the *Bernier*. These two boats came out from Halifax and they'd anchor off Chebucto Head, about half a mile out. They had big lifeboats—one was motorized. They'd fill those things up with coal and barrels of fuel oil. The water was just coming in over the sides of the boat. The boat with the motor towed the other boat. They put a couple of guys in the other one with a big oar down the stern and they'd tow him in. When he got about fifty feet off the rocks, the guy let the tow line come off and that thing just come a beltin' in.

"The guy on the tiller, I can see him yet, leaning on the back with this bloody big oar about thirty feet long trying to steer the thing. There was two rocks he had to go between. They had no way of stopping it.That guy would be free-wheelin' her right into this little gut and then slam! Right up on the rocks! A lot of the time they'd just shoot halfway out of the water and roll over on one side. It was awesome. You had to see it to believe it!"

Then the real work began, winching hundreds of bags of coal up the cliff face for the lighthouse dwelling. The process was often punctuated by breakdowns.

"They had a cable from the top of the cliff down to the boathouse," Don told me. "They used to bring the stuff up to that, on a little skidway. They'd stockpile it there and then a crew would put ten or twelve bags of coal in a sling and hook it to a pulley rig. They'd wind the stuff up and you'd get four slings up and the cable would break. Then the cog on the winch would break and the coal would be all over the place. They had the old burlap bags and the coal would fly out. There was more coal down the face of the cliff! You could have started your own strip mine for Pete's sake!"

Looking back at the whole experience, Don laughed when he thought about it. "When the DOT [Department of Transport] boys showed up with supplies, it was better than the *Ed Sullivan Show!* There

DOT deckhands floating barrels of oil ashore on a calm day at Bon Portage Island in the 1950s.

was more stuff damaged, people in the water and damaged boats and equipment than Hitler caused in the English Channel!"

Getting the stuff ashore on Flint Island presented its own challenges. Alf Hopkins remembered a particular oil delivery that raised his father's blood pressure. As the government supply ship lay off the island, a barge loaded with oil barrels prepared to head in to the station slipway. Brenton Hopkins had an eye on the tide and he called out to the ship: "Listen, it's only half tide," he said. "There's a rock right out in front of the slip. Bring in only half a barge load, 'cause otherwise you're gonna hook up."

Despite the advice, according to Alf, the first mate arrived with the barge, *loaded.* "She was awash. The water was goin' right over the gunwales. And of course they fetched up on this rock and they're solid! They're high and dry. So now there's a big fervour goin' on to get this thing out before all the stuff washed off the deck and overboard."

The mate decided to roll the barrels off the barge to lighten its load. Alf continued the story, shaking his head. "Dad went down the end of the slip and here's these young fellows, eighteen, nineteen years old and they're strugglin' with these barrels through the swells. When the swell would go by, you'd go from five or six feet of water and then you're in only a couple feet of water. These barrels are just barely got their bung out of the water. These guys are slipping on these encrusted rocks, full of algae and they're slippin' and slidin' and these barrels are goin' up and down.

"The old man come down and he hollers, 'Get outta the goddamn water 'fore one of you gets killed, or you lose your legs! The barrel's coming down across your legs if you slip!'"

As if things weren't bad enough, there were still dozens of oil barrels to deliver. The men on the barge rigged up a block and tackle to pass ashore so the barge could be pulled off the rocks. Brenton didn't like the look of the rope he'd received, but the men on the boat said it was just fine. One of the seamen came up the boat ramp to operate the winch in the boathouse—one of those big old flywheeled monsters. Brenton positioned himself to signal the winchman, and as a swell lifted the barge slightly he yelled, "Go Ahead!"

But it turned out that the wave beneath the workboat wasn't big enough to shift the hull off the rock. Brenton yelled for the winchman to slack off. No response. The sailor had "frigged off," when the line went singing tight. "Tight enough to cut you right in two," Alf told me.

Meantime, young Alf was playing in a tide pool about fifty feet from the boat ramp. "I wasn't payin' a lot of attention, because I didn't care what they were doin'. I was only little. But I heard the curse! I turned around just as the old man run across the breakwater and jumped onto the slope on the back side of the breakwater. When he jumped, his hat come off his head. When that rope broke it went between his hat and his head!

"Well, Lord dyin' Jesus, when the old man went up the hill I honestly thought he was gonna do away with that young fella. He tore *such* a strip offa him! It would make a grown man cry! But he didn't touch the young guy. He just said, 'You fly off my island! Don't you step foot onto it again! I don't care if you have to walk on water!'"

Thinking back to that day more than four decades ago, Alf said his father was pretty lucky that day. "There's no doubt in my mind there would have been two pieces settin' there if that rope hadda hit him in the head. You're six or eight inches from death. That does make you cranky, I guess!"

Supply runs were a more leisurely affair at the smaller lights, where a small work boat could nose into a quiet cove and unload. For the kids, watching from a respectful distance, a visit from the government tender was a real event, bringing activity and new faces to remote villages and islands. There might be a handful of hard candy or a chocolate bar from the bosun or the inspector. And afterwards, all those wonderful new supplies to look through!

Helen (Jollimore) Slaunwhite delighted in poking through the big box that held supplies in the little Terence Bay lighthouse, where her father, Hezron Jollimore, was keeper in the 1940s and '50s.

"I remember the steep steps, the smell of wood and the smell of straw," she told me. "At the far end of one wall there was a big box which the supplies were kept in, like the shades for the light. Anything that was breakable was packed in this long box with straw. I remember digging in that straw and investigating and checkin' things over, like the round red globes for the light, wicks and cleaners for the windows."

In the 1960s, the arrival of supplies was an even bigger deal for Valerie and Heather Cameron. Their father, Blair, kept the Beaver Island light, off Port Dufferin on the eastern shore. Valerie laughed and stole a few sidelong glances at her father as she told me how quickly the kids got into the action.

"When supplies would come in we'd open up the boxes and go through them." She paused, and added, "I guess sometimes we'd take a few things and use them in our camps. We'd take a lot of the rags they'd send out and nails. If they had lanterns and things like that we'd take them and we'd put them in our little camps that we'd make. So, we stole a lot of supplies."

"Borrowed," Heather added.

"Ah, yeah, borrowed," Valerie continued. "Of course my father had to account for it. I guess a lot of times he used to think that they shorted him on the supplies. But of course we would get into the boxes before he opened them."

HEYDAY

The labour-intensive work, the night watches, the repairs, the supply deliveries—for more than two centuries these tasks defined the work of the lightkeeper and his family. They were all part of a constant cycle of nightly vigils and daily maintenance necessary to keep equipment operating.

By the early 1960s there were ominous changes in the wind. Electricity, at first embraced as a step towards modern-living on the lights (who else in Canada, aside from lightkeepers and a few isolated rural dwellers, lived without electricity and central heating in the 1960s?), was very soon to mark the end of lightkeeping. Even as the government began to upgrade and modernize lighthouses (including building dozens of dwellings to house the extra lightkeepers hired to fill the mandate for a full slate of three keepers on many sites) they were planning

Cape Sable in its heyday, with (left to right) the foghorn and engine, the base of the original tower, the lighthouse, the keepers' duplex, and the barn.

the installation of automated equipment to replace the lightkeeper. By the early 1970s, many of those extra houses stood empty, as the government reduced staff at lightstations.

For Sid Smith, the best years of lightkeeping came, ironically, just before its demise. "The heyday of lightkeeping to me would have been in the 1960s," he told me. "You had three men. You had your own generated power for electricity. It was always warm out there in the engine room. You had a lot of stuff thrashing around and yeah, I enjoyed the old fog alarm engine and all the mechanisms that went with it."

With the old kerosene light superseded by an electric bulb, there was no need to worry about kerosene flares and the dirty, time-consuming cleanup afterwards. For Sid it was the perfect balance between doing your job and enjoying your life.

Country Island light with Guptill children before the new station replaced the old lighthouse in the background in the mid-1960s.

"It seemed to be you had enough time that you could enjoy the island. It wasn't just work all the time or be on watch all the time. The 1960s were the best years to me as far as lightkeeping was concerned."

Down the eastern shore on Country Island, Jim Guptill sensed that improvements for the lightkeepers might be the beginning of the end.

"The government looked at this lighthouse circumstance and recognized that there needed to be an upgrade. New technology was there—small, lightweight generators—and was all very possible and economically feasible they thought, to go and redo all of the lightstations in Nova Scotia. Country Island was one that was slated for that. In 1964-65, it went from being a one-man station to being a three-man station, and they built a storey-and-a-half house and two bungalows.

"They promoted Dad a classification or two and made him the principal lightkeeper and brought two assistants in to help him out. We started standing twenty-four hour shifts. They tore the old light down. They put on a major fog alarm, the old air-type foghorn. And a radio beacon. Our classification I think was a Morse Code "G" and that was in conjunction with Cranberry Island, Country Island and Sambro. There was five or six of us in that chain. It was a navigational aid. 'Course, satellites have come along and made that obsolete not too long after that, as a matter of fact. *That* changed lightkeeping forever.

"In later years a lot of it was automatic," Jim continued. "With the new setup in the 1970s, the generators would shut down and start up themselves. The A unit would shut down at the end of seven days, at Sunday at noon, and the B unit would start up and would run along with the A unit for a while and then it would pick up the load and the A unit would shut down, and you'd stand there goin', 'Ahh, what do *I* do?'"

Today, Country Island is just a fading shadow of its former self. The last keeper left in 1986. There's no radio beacon anymore. Recently the light has been solarized and the foghorn removed. The Coast Guard burned one of the dilapidated homes in 2004, leaving one decaying house, along with an empty engine room and a concrete lighthouse containing a tiny plastic light powered by a little battery.

On the few remaining staffed lights across the country, the job is much less demanding than it was even in the 1960s—generators provide power for deep-freezers, satellite TV, and clothes dryers. Big fat helicopters descend from the sky at regular intervals to deliver mail, groceries and supplies. Even on the west coast, where militant keepers and active politicians helped stall de-staffing in 1998, the government is slowly whittling away at the keepers' duties, reducing their weather-reporting responsibilities, solarizing lights, and shutting down foghorns.

In Newfoundland, almost all of the offshore stations now stand silent. Some keepers have been re-deployed to mainland stations, where they act as tour guides and heritage interpreters. The Coast Guard has built them little offices where they stand an eight-hour watch, with a computer, fax machine, chemical toilet and a couple of easy chairs. A current Coast Guard handout states that today's keepers are busy "regularly inspecting navigational aids and buildings on site. When they are not logging daily weather conditions or reporting the status of ice floes, lightkeepers are scanning surrounding waters for flares, boats in trouble and other unusual sights."

At quitting time most keepers drive home to their families—apparently between four in the afternoon and eight the following morning there is no weather logging or scanning of the horizon to be done. And so the job has become a "nine-to-five" routine, with no worries about flaring kerosene or broken-down foghorn engines. Those days remain locked away in the memories of a dwindling number of old lightkeepers and their families.

3

A Family Affair

FAMILIES FORMED THE VERY FOUNDATION OF THE LIGHTKEEPING way of life in Nova Scotia and across the Maritimes. From the time a light first shone out over Louisbourg Harbour in 1734 to the last days of staffed stations 250 years later, mothers, fathers, sisters and brothers all worked together to keep the lights burning and horns blaring.

This family tradition set us apart from many European and UK lights, where most keepers worked rotating shifts at their stations, while their families lived ashore. Our neighbours to the south share some of our family lightkeeping history, but after the US Lighthouse Service gave way to the US Coast Guard in 1939, family sites became the domain of bachelor crews that did a hitch on their particular piece of rock and then moved on to another Coast Guard posting.

But in Nova Scotia it wasn't rare to see a little wooden lighthouse perched on a tiny outcrop above a heaving sea, a load of washing flying in the breeze, and kids crawling over the seaweed-covered shoreline, oblivious to what some might see as solitary confinement.

As a child, Kay (Wilson) Ingersoll thought nothing of setting up miniature fishing villages (complete with boats and a tiny lighthouse) in a tide pool on Gannet Rock, just above the

Laundry hangs from the line on tiny Gull Rock, near Lockeport, NS, on a sunny August day in 1945.

A young Kay Wilson stands at Gannet Rock's edge on the Bay of Fundy in the 1930s.

Fundy currents. Her family home sat on a rock smaller than most school playgrounds, and it's almost startling to see photos of young Kay doing normal kid things—playing with her dolls, sitting on a rocking horse, standing on an overturned galvanized washtub—barely out of reach of the restless ocean.

Kay still remembers storms that rocked the old lighthouse, and the lamplight that pushed back the gloom when storm shutters went up over the windows. The sea occasionally smashed into the Wilson's house, sometimes shooting up through the sink drain in the kitchen, but Kay felt safe with her mother and father as the wind roared in the eaves.

The lighthouse as a family operation had certain benefits for both the keeper and his employer. Throughout the nineteenth century and into the twentieth, many lights ran under just one guardian. A wife and kids were indispensable to a man who needed all the help he could get to keep the light burning, run the foghorn, and take care of the day-to-day chores so essential to running a lighthouse. While the Department of Marine and Fisheries' preference for keepers who came with their own free labour may sound a bit mercenary, the Canadian government ran a big service on a small budget. Even as more assistants were hired on in the forties, fifties, and sixties, families continued the form the backbone of the Canadian lighthouse service.

In the course of collecting more than sixty interviews with lighthouse families, I've been struck by the similarities in their experiences. Although characters and personal outlooks differed (as they do everywhere), life on a lightstation had certain constants—the continual fight against the elements, the dangers of raising children in rugged locations, and the routine of keeping lights and foghorns operating.

Today, when former keepers and their children meet with others who lived the lighthouse life, they share a universal connection from that experience. But perhaps the blood ties among lightkeepers are even stronger. In the nineteenth and twentieth centuries, generations of families kept the lightkeeping tradition alive. The Cantwells of Newfoundland are a notable example of this—six generations of the family kept the Cape Spear light near St. John's from the 1840s to 1996.

In Nova Scotia, the job was not just passed from father to son; cousins, uncles, and siblings within families were all involved in the lighthouse business. Take Sid Smith. For half a century, someone in his family looked after the Cape Sable light, at the southwest tip of the

Three lighthouse families at Cape Sable in 1971. Left to right: Morrill Richardson, Sid Smith, Beverly Smith, Betty June (Richardson) Smith, Locke Smith, relief keeper Lovitt Nickerson, his wife Pauline and Evelyn Richardson at far right. Every member of the Smith and Richardson families pictured here worked at one time or another as a lightkeeper.

province. Sid's father, Benjamin, arrived at the station as an assistant in 1929; by 1931 he'd risen to the position of head keeper. He left for a few years after the second world war, returning in 1952 and finally retiring in 1970. In the meantime, Sid's uncle Fred worked as an assistant at Cape Sable in the thirties. Another uncle, Alfred, assisted Benjamin in the thirties and forties. Even Sid's grandfather Enos helped out in the early days.

Lobster for dinner on Gannet Rock. Kay (Wilson) Ingersoll's parents, Donald and Leola, with Vi Wilson (left), wife of principal keeper Arthur Wilson in the 1920s.

But that's not all. Add several cousins and a cousin once removed to the mix, and Sid's two children, Locke and Beverly, as well as their mother Betty June, who all worked as relief keepers at the station. Finally, Sid's cousin Reg brought the family's lighthouse lineage to a close, serving as the Cape's principal keeper from 1979 to 1984. As Sid told me with a grin, "'29 to '84 was the Smiths, I'm afraid!"

Cape Sable also had a link to nearby Bon Portage Island, just eight miles to the west. From 1929 to 1964 the low, scrubby island off Shag Harbour was home to Evelyn and Morrill Richardson and their three children—Anne, Laurie, and Betty June.

Sid Smith met the petite and attractive Betty June while she was working on the mainland. By October 1953 they had married, uniting two lighthouse families. Betty June's great-great-great-great-grandfather had been the first lightkeeper at Yarmouth's Cape Forchu Light, later passing the job to his son John. Great-grandfather Ephraim Larkin lit the little beacon on Stoddart's Island each night from about 1898 to 1937, when he died on the island. An uncle and a cousin of Betty June's worked at lights in the area, and of course there was Betty June's father, Morrill, who not only kept the Bon Portage beacon for thirty-five years, but owned the better part of the island as well.

By now you've likely got the picture. But there's a little more to it. Part of this family involvement came about because keepers often hired their own people for relief and assistant positions. It made sense, as you knew who you were getting and folks were likely to get along. Out on Gannet Rock it was especially important to keep clashes to a minimum. There was literally nowhere to run if you had any issues with your co-worker. Kay Ingersoll told me that the assistants were almost always relatives.

"I don't remember anybody but part of our family being there. It wasn't a problem," she said. "Life, as far as life within the home went, was carried on almost like it would have been if we had lived other places." Kay's father and his assistant had a set routine, going to work on maintenance projects during the day, Kay's mother kept busy with the cooking and cleaning, and little Kay played on the deck and read her books in the sun. And on Sunday, the men had the day off and "my mother dressed up a little bit."

Kay paused for a moment and then concluded "It's surprising how *normal* life was under those circumstances. It really is."

Laurie, Betty June, and Anne Richardson at Bon Portage Island in the 1930s.

WE WOULD SEE OTHER LIGHTS BLOSSOMING IN THE DARK

The best account of family life at a lighthouse appeared on bookstore shelves in 1945. Sixty years later, Evelyn Richardson's *We Keep A Light* continues to delight folks who wonder what it was really like to live in a lighthouse.

Evelyn and her husband, Morrill, involved their children in the day-to-day running of the lighthouse from a very early age. During a visit with her sister and brother-in-law, Anne Wickens cast her mind back seven decades to recall how her parents included her and her siblings in the special time of "lighting up."

"One of my earliest memories is going up the stairs to light the light on the occasions when my father wasn't there to do it *just* at the minute of sunset. I crawled up the very narrow, steep stairs and my mother came behind me carrying my brother, who was a year younger and very heavy and chubby. I was sure I was going to tumble and take her feet out from under her. Then we would go up to the next floor and go around the open stairwell, to another flight. That was worse because part of it was nothing but the open window on the western wall of the lighthouse, and I was always sure I was going to fall through there."

Then came the rigamarole of getting into the lantern. Anne would wait at the bottom of the last ladder, while Evelyn carried little Laurie up, closed the trapdoor, then returned for Anne. With everyone safe in the lantern, Evelyn would put the trapdoor down again so no one could fall down the ladder.

"One of us would have otherwise," Anne said. "We were *that* type of child. Then she would do the evening chores and light the light. She would have a few minutes to pick us up and show us the surrounding territory—the ocean and some of the islands. We would see other lights blossoming in the dark and that was always very interesting."

Anne's mother had a similar affection for their evening ritual. In *We Keep A Light*, she writes, "This hour of 'lighting up' is a time that I enjoy. I love to watch the beams of nearby lights take their places like friendly stars in the twilight. Though I know only one of the keepers, the lights themselves are old friends."

East of Bon Portage, past the "wicked elbow" of the Bay of Fundy, young Bernice (Renehan) Goodick took part in the evening chores as well, helping her father, Douglas, haul kerosene up the wooden stairs in the tall, stone lighthouse at Cape Roseway, sitting at the mouth of Shelburne Harbour.

"At night, we'd watch for Cape Negro to light," Bernice told me. "You'd carry five-gallon cans of kerosene up God knows how many stairs! Dad would light the light with wood alcohol and fill it up with kerosene to keep it burnin' and he would pump the pressure up. Then we'd watch and see Gull Rock light. We lit in sequence. Cape Negro, Cape Roseway, Gull Rock."

Bernice was her father's right-hand girl, always tagging along as Douglas went about his duties. "I was his pet," she told me, "because I was the last child."

Young Reg Smith (upper left) with Ronnie, Freddie, and Shirley in 1944.

Working with Father

Family-run lightstations, for the most part, were happy, productive places. When you treat a lighthouse as your home and the work is everyone's responsibility, you end up with a well-kept station inhabited by a tightly knit family. But working with and for your kin—your father, say—had its own set of challenges from time to time.

Reg Smith moved out to Cape Sable in June, 1944. The quiet lad was just a month shy of his tenth birthday. His father, Albert, who was recently discharged from the army, had landed a job as assistant to his own uncle, Benjamin Smith. Reg's family had ridden the "Blueberry Special" train from Yarmouth to Barrington and then made the short ferry crossing to Cape Sable Island. A bumpy ride in a mail truck got them as far as Clark's Harbour and then they made the short journey to The Hawk—the jumping off point for the Cape Sable light.

It was all a bit mind-boggling for a shy boy who felt like he was travelling to the end of the earth. A short boat ride later, the family found themselves deposited on a sandy beach in a thick fog. Uncle Benjamin was waiting with an ox-drawn cart, and they set off through the dunes with the foghorn blaring louder and louder as they approached the station.

As Reg told me fifty-eight years later, his first impression of Cape Sable as a ten-year-old was, "Where the hell am I and why am I here?" But he didn't have too much time to feel sorry for himself. By the time he was twelve, Reg was helping his father light the large kerosene vapour apparatus in the tower, and when he was thirteen, he stood his first watch for "the old man." He didn't have much choice in the matter. "I done it because he told me I had to. Case closed. And after I turned sixteen, I was told that I was the assistant whether I wanted to be or not."

Albert's pay was not terribly generous—about $120 a month—so the family needed help. That help took the form of a small but able son. For Reg, it was a harsh introduction to the realities of survival.

Even after the family left Cape Sable and moved to Cape Forchu in Yarmouth, where Albert had been promoted to principal keeper, life didn't get any easier for Reg.

"My wages were supposed to be eighty dollars a month, and it was twelve hours a day, seven days a week, 365 days a year," he said. "I never ever did get paid. The years I worked with the old man, my pay went in to help support the family. It wasn't no more than what a fisherman's son was doin' or what a farmers' son was doin'," he said, matter-of-factly. "Today if you hauled a kid thirteen, fourteen years old out of school to go to work in a boat, you better have a damn good explanation how come! But back then it was just the normal thing because wages were lower than you could manage with."

The family raised their own vegetables, kept cows for milk and an ox for work. The work was relentless, and Albert Smith was a tough taskmaster. "The old man had his good days and he had his bad days," Reg recalled. "He had quite a temper and a very short fuse, so ninety per

cent of the time you had to kinda, well, pussyfoot around. I just didn't
want to be around him most of the time."

I got the impression from Reg that it was a bit of a juggling act to
keep his father happy and get the work done. And there were other vari-
ables, including an ornery horse. When Albert decided the ox wasn't fast
enough for farm work, he bought a horse. For some reason, Old Jane
conceived a strong dislike for young Reg.

"If you went in the barn and she saw you comin' out with the collar,
she took off," he said. "Sometimes you had to go to the other end of the
island to get her. On Cape Sable there's a strip of sand that runs about
three miles to the northwest, and she would take off up the beach. Dad
would end up with saddle sores for two or three days from ridin' her
bareback! I couldn't go anywhere near her. She loved to bite, and to be
honest with you, I was scared to death of her. I never did like her and I
think she knew it from the day she landed on the island! I figured the
best way to get along with her was stay away from her altogether.

Sid Smith with his father (and
boss), Benjamin, at Cape Sable
in the 1950s.

"One time Dad had put the harness on her before he went ashore to get the mail and get groceries, and all I had to do was hook her into the wagon. Mum said, 'Well, I'll go along with you,' 'cause with growin' up on a farm, she had quite a good idear how to handle her. She never did make it to the cart! I was on the wagon with the reins in my hand and Old Jane figured it was time to go. She left Mum standin' back in a cloud of dust and me hangin' on for dear life for a mile or so! Then the old man give me a slap on the side 'a the head 'cause the horse was all sweated up. I said 'Boy, I can't win for losin'!'"

Of course, not all father–son lightkeeper relationships had this sort of tension. For Reg's cousin, Sid Smith, working with Dad had certain advantages.

"I could talk him into things I know that nobody else could talk him into," Sid told me with a laugh. "I'd say, 'Well come on Dad, aren't I your little boy?' He would let me go, especially when I was courting my wife. He'd say, 'Well okay, your mother's coming on the island tomorrow and I know between she and myself we can keep things goin' so if you want to go to the mainland for overnight or so, why, go ahead.' That wouldn't have happened if it hadn't been my dad and also if he hadn't thought that Betty June was p'rhaps the nicest little person he'd ever met! I know I wouldn't have gotten away with those kind of things with any other keeper.

"I think the downside of it would be I'm still his boy and he hasn't gotten over it yet. He didn't say, 'You should do this for me,' but you knew that he felt you should not just show respect for him as your employer but as your dad as well. I suppose that had its downside at times but I think the advantages outweighed the disadvantages, really. In fact I know they did."

Imagine working for your father. It's kind of difficult to separate the blood from the boss. But on Country Island, Jim Guptill—who worked as assistant to his father Keith from 1964 to 1974—learned as he matured. He laughed at himself while recalling how it took some time to realize his dad was a pretty smart old fella.

"Through a period in my middle and later teens I thought Dad was a complete moron, but I came to find out that he knew quite a bunch of stuff! But as a teenager you go, 'Oh crap, the old feller's really dumb,' right? But he learned some pile of stuff between the time I was eighteen and the time I was twenty-two! He got his doctorate in a lot of things! By the time I became his assistant pretty much and I moved on there with a new wife, it was *marvellous!* I can't think enough good to say about it, let alone anything bad to say about it. Dad was fair, I thought, and working for a man who you trust and respect and have gotten on fairly well with over the years worked just fine."

THE LIGHTHOUSE AS A HOME

After "Didn't you get lonely out there?" the next question most often asked of a former lightkeeper is, "Did you actually live in the lighthouse?" Most people seem to have an Eddystone-type tower—massive,

"Some were huge, barn-like structures with a lantern on one end of the roof peak." The Beaver Island lighthouse in 1946, when it was one hundred years old.

round and granite—in mind, standing alone on a submerged reef, with the keepers peering out of portholes from tiny round rooms.

Until the 1960s, many Canadian lighthouse families did in fact live in their lighthouses, although these were mostly built on substantial headlands and islands. From the 1840s to the 1940s, the colonial (and later federal) government built several types of combined tower-and-dwelling structures.

Some were huge, barn-like buildings with a lantern on one end of the roof peak. Others incorporated a tower with sloping sides onto the end of a small dwelling. By the 1940s, the Department of Transport favoured a square structure with a small tower and lantern on the apex of the roof.

For children growing up in these towers, life inside the lighthouse was as natural as it would be in a regular, lantern-less house ashore. In her account of her family's years on Bon Portage Island, Evelyn Richardson wrote that the experience permeated all aspects of their young lives, including her kids' representations of "home."

"While most children when learning to draw depict low, squat houses with a door, a window and smoke-billowing chimney, my children's first efforts at drawing a dwelling ran all to height. I was puzzled until I realized that to them home was a lighthouse, like ours small on the ground and running up four stories."

Sixty years later, Evelyn's daughter Anne Wickens told me of her own childhood view of the family home.

"As a little girl, I pictured lighthouses, all lighthouses, with people living in them. Cape Sable was a great big tall needle of a lighthouse and I thought, well, there would be little boys and girls sleeping on all of the stories going up to the lantern, as Laurie and I did when we got a little older. I would look over at Great-Grandpa Larkin's light on the next island to us [Stoddart's Island]. It was just a little one-storey light and I would think about my little half-aunt and half-uncle who were younger than I, sleeping in that, and it was a great blow to me when I found out that they didn't!"

Meanwhile, back at Bon Portage, the lighthouse could truly be described as a "family" lighthouse, with bedrooms in the lower floors of the tower, and the rest of the structure devoted to a living room and kitchen. Anne later wrote a description of her childhood home for a story in *The Lightkeeper*, the journal of the Nova Scotia Lighthouse Preservation Society.

> The lighthouse, as erected by the Government [in 1874], consisted of a fine, full-sized, fieldstone cellar; the tower, slanting inward all the way to the lantern on top; a northward- jutting ell. These provided two fair-sized rooms and a porch the full width of the ground floor. This porch, alas, opened to the north with a wide door.

> The chief problem was that the first keeper, Will Wrayton, had seven small children. Another man, at least in winter, was a necessity that had to be fitted in *somewhere*. Will complained that they were "crawling all over each other like maggots." With or without official permission, he added a kitchen ell on a stone foundation. The kitchen was complete with closet—the only closet in the house—and a door opening to the south, to milder winds, usually less violent than the northern ones. The new kitchen being below the original structure, Will built steps to the level of the former porch. Such flights, especially in a kitchen, were known as 'woman killers'. Part of the former porch was then a passage to the original kitchen; the eastern part of a pantry. In winter, the pantry advanced to the status of a refrigerator.

> Our father, after wrestling with the results of Will's endeavours, always declared that no Irishman should ever be permitted to build *anything*. (He was partly of Irish descent himself.) Nothing Will built was straight, or square, or level; nevertheless, I feel he had the right idea.

By the time the Richardsons moved into the Bon Portage lighthouse in 1929, the old structure had weathered fifty-five years of wind, salt spray, and blistering sun. As Evelyn noted with some resignation, first impressions of their new home were not entirely pleasing: "Things looked better, of course, in the bright sunshine of a new day, but it would have taken more than a good night's sleep and a beautiful morning to alter the hard fact that the lighthouse, as a home, was inconvenient, gloomy, and very much in need of repairs, and that mountains of work lay before us, both indoors and out."

Evelyn also bemoaned the lack of a telephone or two-way radio for communication with the shore. (Some New Zealand lights had telephones in the 1880s!) It wasn't until after *We Keep A Light* was published in 1945 that the government finally installed a radiophone at Bon Portage.

Lack of amenities was a common problem facing keepers dealing with a government that had tight purse strings. Back in 1902, a terse letter from Ottawa noted that in no uncertain terms would the department supply bathroom hot water connections for the lightkeeper at Vancouver's Brockton Point. The memo went on to state that "Hot water in a bath room is considered a luxury, and if keepers desire luxuries, they must pay for them themselves." Indeed, how could the keeper have the audacity to ask for hot water when his was "the only lighthouse in the Dominion that has a bathroom of *any kind* supplied to it"?

So, living conditions in many of these quaint, picturesque old towers left much to be desired. Russ Latimer still remembers moving to the Jerseyman Island lighthouse off Isle Madame in Cape Breton in 1930, and discovering "the terrible condition of the house." It was a similar structure to the Bon Portage light, located slightly above a low beach, about a kilometre and a half from the village of Arichat. For ten-year-old Russ, the family's new digs were a bit of an adventure, but for his mother Dorothy, brought up in London "in a rather comfortable home," this was not impressive.

"She only ever had one reference to the lighthouse," Russ told me, laughing. "She called it the 'God-forsaken hole'! That's what I remember all the years I knew her. And even after she left there and lived in a home in Sydney, she marvelled at the fact she brought up her four sons and they were all successful, but what a God-forsaken hole that was!"

Dorothy Latimer may have had good reason to hold that view. As Russ notes, the government didn't put much thought into "people comforts when they built those towers! Ours was thinly sheathed on the inside with rough boards they had wallpapered. And because the tower part was tapered, the wallpaper had a habit of leaving the wall and then flapping in the wind, so it was a pretty breezy place to live!"

Despite her misgivings, Dorothy made the best of her time in the lighthouse, joining the T. Eaton Company's "Home-Lover's" club, where an easy payment of five dollars a month allowed her to buy new wallpaper and curtains and make the best of a bad living situation.

It was always a struggle in these isolated and exposed places to keep a house warm and comfortable. Out on Cape Sable, the keepers lived in a house separate from the light. It was a rambling old duplex, built in 1910, and as Sid Smith remembered, "it was an awful old thing when you stop and think of it!" Built on a high foundation, the house took easterly and westerly winds broadside. After an easterly storm, the wind sometimes lulled and then veered to the west. Then you'd hear "this awful crunch!" The house, formerly leaning to the west in an easterly gale, would suddenly shift in the opposite direction. "All the doors that normally would open now wouldn't open, and all that ones that wouldn't open before, would fly open!"

But for Sid and his siblings, it was all a great adventure, and he has fond memories of dragging a mattress downstairs to sleep by the stove, while his mother hung up blankets to keep the drafts out and his father Benjamin lugged coal to keep the fire going.

In the 1950s and '60s, the Canadian Government embarked on a program of modernization, building new homes for keepers and their families and installing generators for power. Not many missed the old days, but even into the 1960s, some keepers were still caught in a time warp.

Wick Lent started lightkeeping on Brier Island, at the end of Digby Neck in the late '50s. After settling in on the island's Grand Passage lighthouse, he noticed that no matter how hot the stove was, he couldn't keep heat in the house.

"You could stand with your butt against the kitchen stove and your ears and your belly would freeze," Wick told me as we sat in his basement apartment in New Minas on a bitter winter day. "So I went investigating. When I went up the back stairs I could look right straight through the attic and see the bell buoy in the passage out in front of the house! That's what I was trying to heat—Grand Passage! It was the eaves trough had sagged with dirt, never been cleaned out. I went to work stuffin' in oakum and tore up boards that was there and nailed them on for to hold it down. Finally I got the house nice and warm!"

Conditions didn't improve much after Wick and his wife Madeline transferred to the island's Western Light. Two new houses were in planning stages, but for the time being they had to inhabit an ancient, leaky dwelling. Madeline set out pots to catch the drips, arranging them so that they'd play a tune.

In addition, there was no electricity in the old house, even though the engine room and lighthouse had been recently wired. Wick said it "was comical. You'd see somebody that used an electric razor if they wanted to shave, you'd see them going with a basket, with a towel over it heading for the lighthouse to start up the big diesel engine to have a shave!"

With the completion of a comfortable new bungalow in the mid-sixties, the Lents were set to enter the twentieth century when another keeper came to the station and decided *he* wanted the new house. No matter, Wick and Madeline weren't troubled, as the government completed a large duplex soon after. As Wick told me, it was the right move for them, but not for the new keeper's family. "Were they ever sorry, because you couldn't heat that bungalow to save your soul, the hell you couldn't!" he said with a grin.

In the final years of staffed lights in the Maritimes, living in a lightstation house was like living in any comfortable mainland home, with electricity, central heating, microwave ovens, and television. But until 1996 there was one notable exception—Gannet Rock.

When I arrived on Gannet, the old concrete house, built during the Depression, was not insulated, didn't have central heating, and man! Was it cold in the winter! With three oil stoves running full bore, the areas around the stoves were tolerable. But the upstairs bathroom, with only a tiny baseboard heater, was like a crypt, where the toilet seat met your bottom in a distinctly icy embrace.

We had indoor storm windows to put in during the cold months, and the water condensing and freezing on the inside formed amazing

patterns resembling lush tropical growth. But with a screeching north wind, a -50 degree wind chill, and the foghorn blowing into the tendrils of sea smoke, tropical was only a desperate dream.

It was just as well the families had been moved off Gannet in the 1950s, leaving us hardy bachelor crews to suffer out the winters.

Keepers were jacks of all trades. Morrill and Laurie Richardson work on a make-and-break engine that will power Evelyn's washing machine on Bon Portage Island.

SET FOR LIFE

Cramped and draughty lighthouses aside, by most accounts, family life was good on a lightstation. Adversity brought family members closer together—you had to depend on each other for survival, entertainment and plain old company.

That way of life is disappearing, now that most of us live in or near cities, with both parents working, kids in daycare, and video games and the internet making us more insular than we ever were living on farms and in fishing villages and lighthouses.

The life didn't bother Russ Latimer. Primitive living conditions and lack of playtime were a novelty to a lad who loved messing around in boats. When he wasn't "preparing kindling wood, carrying coal and kerosene, cleaning lamp chimneys and looking after the hens and the pig and the cattle," Russ was on the water, rowing to school in the lap-strake boats his father built. He claimed that growing up on Jerseyman stood him in good stead for what was to come.

"I sometimes look back, and particularly I hear a lot about young people with nothing to do and they get in trouble through idleness. Well, we never experienced that! There was no idleness. I also believe it was a tremendous base. You seemed to be able to cope with most anything. For example, if you had a minor accident, if you broke an oar in the boat, you paddled ashore or you were smart enough to carry three oars. You were your own sort of fellow and nothing seemed to be too large to cope with." But when it came time to leave the island, Russ was a bit worried: "I particularly noticed when I left home and came to Halifax, that gosh, what a little world I lived in! What must it be like out there and how would I compete with all the smart people I'm gonna meet?"

It turned out that Russ did pretty well for himself. He left home in 1939, joining a British-registered cable ship. After two years he came ashore to study marine radio communications. By 1942, with a newly minted certificate of radio proficiency, Russ joined the Canadian Merchant Marine as a radio officer. For more than a decade, he sailed the waters of the world, relishing every moment. When I talked to him almost half a century after coming ashore and going into business for himself, Russ brought the whole journey full circle to his life on Jerseyman Island.

"I was always a bit of a loner, and I wonder if that came upon me as a result of living on the island, or if this was my style of living. That's why I enjoyed going to sea so well. I remember a time we were on a beautiful T2 tanker. She was done up so nice and I joined her in Portland, Maine. We sailed via the Cape of Good Hope to Abu Dhabi in the Persian Gulf, and I remember standing alongside the skipper on the bridge one beautiful day in the Indian Ocean. He said 'God, Sparks, wouldn't it be nice to see the end of this?'

"'Sir,' I says, "This is so beautiful it wouldn't matter to me if we never arrived in port!'

"'Something wrong with you!' he said. I suppose that's why I also enjoyed Jerseyman Island and the boats."

THAT LIGHTHOUSE WAS HOPPING!

For the Cleveland family, life was a busy, interesting and joyous affair. From 1932 to 1957 the McNabs Island lighthouse (not to be confused with the Maugher's Beach light on the same island) was home to Colin and Glennie Cleveland and their seven children. Colin had been a fisherman and worked at the sugar and oil refineries in Dartmouth. As a veteran of World War One, he was a preferred candidate for the job at the McNabs Island lighthouse.

The family wasn't isolated—a short boat ride could take you to the biggest city in the region, or over to Eastern Passage, where the girls went to school. The entire island, 4.8 kilometres (three miles) long, became a playground for daughters Joan and Faye. But the centre of their life was family and home. Faye remembers her father waking her up in the morning, and standing her on some newspapers on the kitchen stove's water tank, to get her warmed up. After a breakfast of hot porridge, it was time to suit up for the boat ride to school in Shearwater.

Colin's work kept him close to home—polishing and lighting the

The Cleveland family on McNabs Island in 1942.

reflector lamp in the lantern mounted on the house, clearing land for gardens and taking care of his livestock. Joan remembers him as a serene man, happy with his world of lighting lamps, cutting wood and keeping the lighthouse spic and span. He liked to sing, too. Faye remembers her father up on scaffolding, painting away, and belting out verse after verse of "Onward Christian Soldiers."

He wasn't beyond a little fun, though. One day when Faye had her friend Harold over, the boy decided he'd like to sneak a smoke, so he headed over to the dog house to have a few puffs. Later Faye and Harold returned to the lighthouse, where Colin carefully looked at Harold and drawled, "Lad, I believe you were smokin'!" With grudging admiration, Harold later told Faye, "Your father's got some sniffer on him!"

During wartime, the island was a beehive of activity, with soldiers and officers staffing several forts. Despite the war, it was a happy time for the Cleveland family. "The soldiers all came down to the house," Joan told me. "Nothing to do with the daughters who lived there, I don't suppose! They would bring guitars and violins and one fella had a saxophone and there was always music. There was always fun, carrying on, stories to be told and it was just a going concern all the time. Those same soldiers taught my sister Joyce and I how to dance with all this music going on. So what were we, nine and ten years old? God bless them, they saw that we learned to dance."

Today, the Cleveland kids are spread all over Canada and the US. But the family has stayed tight, united by their close family ties on McNabs Island. Faye thought for a moment, then summed it all up.

"It all revolved around our parents. Mum was the instigator of getting us out into the world, prodding us to do things, like suggesting I move to California with my family. Mum liked the adventure and tried to get the adventure through to us kids. Dad would have been quite happy to be stationary. They were a good complement to each other. Dad would make sure we got the education, but Mum was the one pushing us out into the world to make something of ourselves."

4

Lighthouse Women

Officially, lightkeeping was always the domain of men. Technical and labour-intensive by nature, the work was seen by lighthouse authorities of various eras as eminently suited to the male sex. At the same time, lighthouse administrators were canny enough to know that a man with a wife (and a family) came with built-in labour. No need to hire an assistant when the wife and kids could work for free!

As early as 1847, surveyor Captain W. F. W. Owens submitted a report to the Commissioners of Lighthouses, noting, "Keepers of all lighthouses should be married men, and the wives be instructed in the duties as well as the husbands for the whole work within the buildings is capable of being performed by women."

Maggie Boutilier could turn her hand to any task on Croucher's Island.

It would be misleading, though, to say that the role of women in lightkeeping was purely a function of being attached to their husbands. Many women were prime movers in encouraging their spouses to apply for a lightkeeping job. Others willingly moved to isolated lights and shared in the duties of lighthouse life. A few even took over after their husbands died, living out the rest of their working lives as paid keepers.

Such was the case for Eliza Campbell. After her husband drowned in 1942, she assumed duties at Scatarie Island's west light, across the water from Main-a-Dieu, Cape Breton. She raised three children at the lighthouse, while maintaining a home and the all-important beacon mounted on its roof. Eliza Campbell left the island reluctantly, when she retired in 1963.

Eliza was a bit of an oddity in a male-dominated lightkeeping world. Very few Canadian women have been recognized for their contributions to lighthouse life or safety at sea. It's a different situation in the United States, were a number of high-profile female lightkeepers have been documented and lauded.

Maryland's Fannie Salter kept the Turkey Point light for more than two decades. Katie Walker lived on a tiny reef light in New York Harbour for thirty-four years, saving more than fifty lives during her tenure as lightkeeper.

Ida Lewis took over duties at Lime Rock in Rhode Island's Newport Harbour at the tender age of sixteen. As Candace Flemming writes in her book *Women of the Lights*, Ida, "in running and maintaining the lighthouse…found a freedom she had never known before. No longer was she limited to the traditional female roles of cooking and housekeeping. Now, Ida was doing a man's job."

Of the smattering of Canadian lighthouse women who have been researched and written about, only one has received any notable attention. Mary Hichens moved to Seal Island, off the southwest tip of Nova Scotia, in 1823. The island had a deadly reputation as a killer of ships and sailors—from the early eighteenth century to the mid-twentieth century, hundreds of vessels came to grief on its fog and surf-wrapped shores. The story goes that Mary, the daughter of a Barrington preacher, persuaded her husband to settle there after hearing horrific stories of wreckage and decaying bodies washed ashore on the island.

Mary's husband Richard, along with Edmund Crowell, set up a lifesaving station on the island. For the next eight years, the men kept busy, pulling survivors from the frigid waters around Seal Island and providing shelter and food for those lucky enough to be tossed ashore. But as the popular story goes, these efforts weren't enough for Mary. She informed her husband that a lighthouse was the *best* way to protect mariners from Seal Island's dangers.

Richard Hichens, lobbied by his wife about the virtues of a guiding light on the island, began to lobby the provincial government. With the support of Lieutenant Governor Sir James Kempt and Samuel Cunard (at that time the head of the provincial lighthouse commission and later the founder of the famous shipping line that still bears his name), the Nova Scotia House of Assembly voted the sum of £1000 to build a light-house. Workers completed the massive timber structure in 1831.

Although Mary Hichens never became a lightkeeper—her husband and his lifesaving partner Edmund Crowell took turns maintaining the light—she is widely recognized as Nova Scotia's and Canada's only light-house heroine. If she hadn't put the bug in her husband's ear about a light-house, many more hapless sailors would have died on Seal Island's shores.

The Canadian Coast Guard officially recognized Mary Hichens in 1985, when they named a sixty-four-metre search-and-rescue vessel after her. (The recognition didn't last long—the Coast Guard decom-missioned and sold the *Mary Hichens* off in 2000.)

But what of the legions of unrecognized lighthouse women in Nova Scotia? Most just went about their business, assisting their husbands, teaching their children, and running their households. It was *not* an easy life. Cut off from friends and family, there was no escape for these women from the workaday drudgery of laundry, cooking and cleaning—especially in the days before electricity. At best there was limited social contact with other women or friends and family ashore. No church, no socials. Just miles of ocean and stacks of work.

Some women couldn't stand lighthouse life. Russ Latimer's mother, Dorothy, remember, never called Jerseyman Island anything other than

Dale (Matthews) Veinot wasn't crazy about life on Georges Island as a child.

"that God-forsaken hole!" As a child Dale Veinot "hated" being confined on tiny Georges Island in Halifax Harbour. For Marie (Palmer) Stevens, life at Owl's Head on the eastern shore was "horrible."

Others embraced the experience. Lynne Wolfe loved raising her three kids on West Ironbound and Mosher islands at the entrance to the LaHave River, where family life was "very close, because that was all you had."

For Kay Major, who came to the lights after her own kids were grown, "it was just like life startin' over again." It was 1976 when her husband Harry was appointed head keeper at Betty's Island, near Terence Bay.

"Me and my husband alone," Kay told me. "No family. It was surprising after almost thirty-seven years of marriage to turn around and say, I'm starting all over with my husband. It was nice."

Whether life on the lights was complete drudgery or a new start, women formed the backbone of lightkeeping in Nova Scotia and across Canada right until the end. Women were the glue that kept families together, while fathers tended the light and farmed and fished off their little islands. Many sacrificed their ties ashore to maintain the family unit, and lighthouse kids—even the Palmer girls, who really didn't like life at Owl's Head—to this day remember how Mum always had a warm house and good food on the table, despite the plethora of tasks demanding her attention.

Women on the lights today are just as likely to be lightkeepers themselves (although not, of course, in Nova Scotia, now that our beacons are automated and de-peopled). One of the last principal keepers at Cape Forchu, the province's final light to close, was a woman. In early 2005, ten out of twenty-seven staffed lightstations in British Columbia had female assistant keepers. Some worked with their husbands and a few did relief work up and down the coast. Recently the Coast Guard posted a competition for lightkeepers in Newfoundland, open only to female Newfoundlanders.

Times have changed for the better on the few remaining staffed lights across the country, but for the better part of 260 years, the *unpaid* toil and trouble of hundreds of women formed the core of our lighthouse system.

Lighthouse life on Betty's Island meant a new start for Harry and Kay Major.

THAT'S NOT MEN'S WORK!

For many years and for many women, lightkeeping was a microcosm of the larger world. Husbands got the job, received the pay and the glory. Women toiled behind the scenes. As Fiona Marshall notes in her Master's thesis on Evelyn Richardson's contributions to lightkeeping, local history, and environmental conservation, lightstation women "lived and worked in an environment that for generations had been oriented toward men, dominated by men and regulated by men."

There is a flip side to this observation. Many women came to take the lead role in the running of their lighthouses in the days before women were even considered for paid lightkeeping positions. Grace (Shatford) Cahill's mother was one such person.

Flora and Oliver Shatford lived in the Greens Point lighthouse near Hubbards, on the South Shore, from 1912 to 1944. Along with raising eleven kids in the tiny wooden lighthouse, doing the cooking, darning the socks, washing the clothes, and doing any number of other daily domestic chores, Flora did most of the lightkeeping.

I visited her daughter, Grace, in early 2002. She'd been in the hospital for a long stretch before my visit and she wasn't feeling tip-top. But her sharp tongue revealed that she had plenty of energy and opinions. Sitting in a rocker next to her shiny oil stove, Grace cast her mind back eighty years, remembering her mother climbing the stairs to light the kerosene lamp within the lens each night. "She used to polish the brass every day," she told me. "In the winter it was so cold up there and she used to have to go up and put rubbin' alcohol to get the glasses clear."

I asked Grace what her father, the lightkeeper, was doing while her mum took care of the light. She answered me sharply, saying, "Well, that's indoor work. That's not men's work! That's indoor work!" So while Flora took care of the lamps and lens, Oliver Shatford "worked at different things. He was quite a man! He was the assessor and he was the secretary of the school. He was secretary of the [Masonic] Lodge and he was lookin' after women that lost their husbands—it used to be called Mother's Allowance. After the old age pension came in he had to look after that. He was a man was always doin' somethin' and never got nothin' for it!"

In the evenings, Oliver sat in his rocking chair with two or three kids on his lap, singing songs. But there was no relaxing for Flora, as her daughter remembers. "Mama didn't. Mama was always doin' *somethin'*." Grace loved both her mother and her father, but judging by her reminiscences, it seems that Flora was the light in the lighthouse—she even kept a lamp burning in a window at night as a beacon for her family as they returned home from Hubbards.

The division of labour on Bon Portage Island was considerably different. When Evelyn and Morrill Richardson arrived on the 243-hectare (600-acre) strip of spruce, swamp, and rock in 1929, the couple dove into lightkeeping life with gusto. Although Evelyn was in charge of most of the domestic duties, she and Morrill worked as a team on the family's lighthouse and farm—making hay and silage, shearing sheep, and occasionally even duck hunting together.

The light remained "the nucleus" of the Richardsons' job, though, and Evelyn learned to operate the light if Morrill was busy elsewhere. "It often comes about," she wrote in *We Keep a Light*, "that Morrill is not able to be home at sunset to 'light up,' and I act as substitute lightkeeper. After the lamps have been lit, and the mechanism that revolves the light is set in motion, I must stay for some time in the lantern, as we call the glass-and-metal enclosure that contains the light apparatus and through which the beams of the lamp are visible from the sea. This is to make certain that all is operating smoothly, since any flaw in the performance is most apt to appear when the mechanism starts."

Evelyn also learned to keep the necessary logbooks and operate the hand-pumped foghorn. This meant staying close to an open door in foggy weather and, at the sound of a ship's horn, dropping everything to run to the shore and give an answering blast. This duty often interfered with domestic chores, and Evelyn wrote that the "ultimate exasperation is, I think, to sit on the foghorn beside the lighthouse and give the necessary answering toots to some sailing vessel tacking back and forth outside the Point, in an almost complete calm, while dinner gets cold or housework goes undone for hours."

LIGHTHOUSEKEEPING
AND HOUSEKEEPING

A Gannet's-eye-view of Gannet Rock, a great place to bring up a child, according to Kay (Wilson) Ingersoll.

Keeping the household in order was an added challenge when your house was stuck on a speck of rock in the middle of the Bay of Fundy. A few months before Evelyn and Morrill Richardson were unpacking their bags and surveying their domain on Bon Portage Island, Donald and Leola Wilson were setting up house on tiny Gannet Rock. It was December 1928, and Leola was faced with the task of raising her two-month-old daughter Kathleen (Kay) on a wave-washed rock barely bigger than the dwelling and tower anchored to it.

She rose to the challenge. For the first three years the family lived in a leaky old brick house attached to the light tower. It was decrepit enough that it had to be braced by heavy timbers to keep it from falling over, and leaky enough that seawater dripped on Leola's pots that hung on the kitchen walls.

Then, around 1930, came the big upheaval. The government decided to demolish the old brick structure (by hand, with pickaxes and sledgehammers!) and construct a new concrete affair for Gannet's keepers. As Kay remembered, the family "received word on Friday to move out of the house, and have meals ready for the men by Monday morning. On Monday they began to flatten the old house."

The job of preparing meals for twelve workmen fell to Kay's mother. Over the years, it came to be a regular duty as various work gangs descended on the rock, squeezing into the lighthouse for their week-long stints of work. (Most went ashore for a break on the weekends.)

Six decades later, Kay marveled at the way her mother was able to feed hungry workers, while taking care of her own family. She saved menus from a summer-long work project when men came to repair storm damage to the lighthouse, and she read them to me during a visit:

"For breakfast—now this was all served out in the cookhouse— there were beans, bacon and eggs, cereal, toast, doughnuts, molasses and jam, and dried, stewed fruit. Monday was boiled dinner and pudding. Tuesday was a fish dinner. Wednesday, ham. Thursday a stew with dessert. There was dessert for all this. Friday, fish, and Sunday, roast meat. What a lot of work! Dad would peel a pail of potatoes each day, and Mum had a roaster of leftovers to use for night lunches."

As if that wasn't enough, the crew from the nearby lifesaving station on Outer Wood Island made regular visits to the rock to deliver supplies and water—they too joined the hungry throng.

It was always a challenge to lay in enough provisions. Kay showed me one of her mother's lists of annual supplies brought by the government supply ship *Dollard*.

Four barrels of flour
One barrel of sugar, about 380 pounds
Two sixty-pound tubs of shortening
One barrel hard tack
Two boxes of crackers
One barrel broken biscuits (cookies)
Two cases of corned beef
Cases of vegetables: corn, peas, tomatoes, beans

One hundred-pound bag of dried beans
One hundred pounds of bean pork
Twelve cases of canned milk [forty-eight cans in a case]
One pound each of pepper, cinnamon, cloves, allspice, ginger
Twenty-five pounds of soda, which was used for cleaning
Ten pounds of cream of tartar
Ten pounds of cocoa
Twenty-five pounds of tea
Ten pounds of coconut
Fifteen pounds of oatmeal
Twenty pounds of jam
One case each dried prunes, apples, peaches
Ten gallons of molasses
One case of dates
One case of raisins
A hundred pounds of salt, used for salting fish and meat

It was an incredible amount of food, but keeping a six-month supply on hand was crucial when you could be cut off for weeks or months, as wind and waves turned Gannet into a tiny prison. Thanks to Leola's efforts, it was far from that. Kay remembered on Sundays the lightkeepers took the day off and Leola dressed up a little and made a special dinner for the family.

On the weekends the men got to listen to the ball game on the Radiola, but after four o'clock it was time for Leola and the assistant keeper's wife to have their turn, putting on two pairs of earphones to listen to the soap opera *Today's Children*, "and crochet and tell everyone else to keep *still* so they could hear!" Kay laughed as she looked back.

SIXTEEN SMILEYS

Life on tiny Gannet Rock would have been a challenge for Muriel Smiley. Today, Muriel lives in Liverpool with her daughter, who runs a daycare centre out of her home. Lively and noisy during the school year, it seems fitting place to live, seeing as Muriel raised *fourteen* children of her own. (There just wouldn't be enough room for them all on Gannet!) I try to picture this calm, smiling woman who's pushing eighty but looks at least ten years younger, keeping track of a bevy of kids who didn't go away at the end of the day.

Muriel and her husband Doug lived at the Beaver Harbour Head lighthouse on Nova Scotia's eastern shore in the 1950s. They'd made a brief stab at life on nearby Beaver Island in 1946, but Muriel had problems with the island's hard water. They only stayed for two months. Six years later, when the chance came for a mainland light, Muriel suggested she put Doug's name in for it. "You're only wasting your time," he said.

"It's only an envelope and a stamp!" his wife countered.

It was worth the time and the cost of a stamp. Doug got the job, and in October 1952 the family moved to Beaver Harbour Head, beginning a thirty-five-year career on the lights. Their new home was a neat, square house with a light on top, at the cliff's edge. Although it was a mainland light, you couldn't drive to it. Instead, the family car got parked on the main road, and the Smileys walked the remaining two kilometres to the house.

By this time Muriel had four children but no electricity and no indoor plumbing. She took it all in stride, but admitted it took some doing to get used to "the old scrub boards, the old bathtubs, and the stove, which was very unique." It was an old, cranky Waterloo, already a century-old antique in 1952, with an oven on its chimney. It took some doing to figure out how much coal to feed it and which drafts to open and close to get the best oven temperature.

Young Virginia Smiley at the Beaver Harbour Head lighthouse "school."

Muriel eventually mastered the stove, but there were other things cooking. By 1959 there were *eight* kids in the family and it was getting to be too much to raise little ones and educate the older children through correspondence. It was time for a move.

Luckily, there was a position open at the Medway Head light near Liverpool. There was a school nearby, other children for the Smiley kids to play with, and, best of all, electricity! "First thing I bought was a washer!" Muriel remembered, laughing. Still, they did without an indoor toilet for a few years, and family members had to make the trek to the outhouse, rain or shine, to answer nature's call. After a few years, workmen from the Department of Transport arrived to install a much-anticipated indoor toilet.

It so happened that the day the men arrived was the day Lee Harvey Oswald pulled the trigger and John F. Kennedy slumped in the seat of his limousine as his motorcade passed through Dealey Plaza in Dallas. Muriel remembers the workmen measuring the space for the toilet, running down to watch the news on the television, running outside to check out the site for the septic field, and running back in again to gape at the TV. There wasn't a lot of progress on the toilet that day—J. F. K. took precedence.

The indoor toilet was a blessing, as the Smiley family soon swelled to a grand total of sixteen. By the time child number fourteen had arrived, the older ones had grown up and were on their own, so there were never more than eight kids at a time in the house. But eight or fourteen—it didn't matter to Muriel. "I wasn't one to have everything spotless," she told me. "Children would be playing, somebody would come in, toys could be all over the floor, but I didn't call that *dirty*." She laughed. "People used to ask me if I had to count their little boots in the nighttime to see if they were all in!"

I USED TO CLIMB THE TOWER AND CRY

It wasn't a life that appealed to all women. During the Depression years any job with a regular paycheque was good for a family, but that didn't mean it was easy. Lighthouse life provided precious little time for leisure or solitude.

Etta Palmer was pleased when her husband got a job at the Owl's Head light, near Clam Bay on the eastern shore in the early 1920s. It meant the whole family would be together after her husband John's years of working as a cook at sea and in the woods. It also meant a steady (if very modest) paycheque. But with eight children to look after on the edge of a granite cliff more than six kilometres from the nearest road, Etta had her hands full.

There was no time to mess around. Etta had a house to run. As her daughter Marie explained to me, "Mother was the boss. What Mother said, you did, or else!"

Marie's sister Melda says their mother kept a pretty close eye on her kids at playtime. "We couldn't play at the light. We'd fall right over in the water. We used to have to go down over the hill where there were flat lands and beaches. We weren't allowed to go near the water. Just put your feet in, that's it! It must have been an awful worry, now that I'm older and think about me mother out there with all them kids. She kept a very tight rein on us!"

I asked Melda how well her mother coped with the stresses of taking care of eight kids so close to the sea and other dangers. She thought for a moment. Then she laughed.

"Well, I suppose if she had lived in a normal place, she might have been a normal person! But stuck out there with all them kids? Oohh, she was kinda cranky at times! It must have been horrible. When you got all that many kids, you can't have too much time for just settin' down and relaxin'.

"Every time we'd growl and grumble 'bout bein' there she used to tell us we were lucky to have a roof over our head. Which I guess we were. That was in the Depression. She didn't have too much sympathy on us, so I don't know how she felt herself. She wasn't about to give her feelings away."

Not many lighthouse women gave their feelings away when I talked with them. I didn't pry for personal information, but sometimes it was evident that I'd touched a nerve or helped dredge up a painful memory. Some people just didn't want to talk too much about the nitty gritty. But sometimes it was there, between the lines.

Marjorie Fairservice moved out to Sambro Island in 1964, when her husband John got a job as assistant keeper. It was a good life for John. He'd been in the navy, and he was used to isolation and routine. There were two other lightkeepers, and the men were always busy with painting, mowing, and working on engines and other watch-related duties.

It was a different kettle of fish for the sociable Marjorie. With three small kids and cut off from family ashore, the first few years on Sambro Island were pretty rough. After a fast-paced life on the mainland, everything seemed to stop. There were only two neighbours in a tiny world surrounded by the sea. John was wrapped up in the man's world of lightkeeping. To make matters worse, the mainland was tantalizingly close—about a kilometre and a half away—yet maddeningly unreachable when winter storms confined the family to the house.

Direct and blunt, Marjorie doesn't mince words when she talks about the first year on the island. "I hated it," she told me. Taking her little daughter Kelly with her, she'd "climb the tower and cry." Every time a boat stopped in at the island, Marjorie would try to get ashore. "It didn't matter how rough it was!"

After a while she learned to cope with the isolation. There were three energetic kids to look after—brother Philip dropped his two sisters off on a tide-washed rock one day and left them there. Deidre liked to hang over the edge of the lighthouse balcony. One day Kelly found paint cans containing yellow highway paint washed up on the beach— Marjorie found the kids "paintin' each other and the rocks."

Grey hairs for Marjorie, but the kids survived. As the years passed, more trips ashore to visit friends and family helped ease the stress of isolation. Then, in the early 1970s, Marjorie became an assistant lightkeeper herself, beating out six male applicants for the position. But there was a speedbump on the road to the position. The man who came in second on the competition got the job. Incensed, Marjorie consulted a lawyer and called the Coast Guard. The department decided to run another competition. Marjorie won. The job was hers.

Life got a little better. As Kelly told me, if her mother was going to be "miserable on an island, she might as well get paid for it!"

Still, it was a challenge to work with her husband, especially since he was the boss. As Marjorie remembered, "it did have its ups and downs, but if things got too rough and I didn't want to do a job anymore, I just told John I was gonna resign and *he'd* go and do the job!"

Sitting next to his wife on the couch at their daughter Kelly's home, John added, "I seen her pay cheque comin' in, so I didn't want to fire her, that's for sure!" Later, Kelly added, "Working for Dad? My mother deserves a medal."

At the end of my visit with Kelly and her folks I asked Marjorie what the *best* of part of living on Sambro Island had been. She answered without hesitation.

"Leaving! That was the best part. I was really glad when everything was packed and off of there. I knew I had another job. I was working in the office at the Coast Guard, which I knew wasn't gonna last long 'cause I didn't like it and I knew I was gonna get a job at Eddy Point at the lighthouse monitoring station."

Marjorie later went on to become principal keeper at Yarmouth's Cape Forchu lighthouse, overseeing the monitoring system for more than twenty automated lights. Town was just a ten-minute drive away. There were lots of visitors. She was the boss. It was light years away from the early days when a lonely mother climbed the old stone tower on Sambro Island to cry and wish for a better life somewhere else.

EVELYN RICHARDSON: AN ENDURING BRILLIANCE

Whether they wanted a better life or not, lighthouse women were invariably strong and dedicated. Three names stand out to me, united in their amazing capacity to provide for their families and survive in primitive and harsh environments. That's not to say that *all* of these women enjoyed the life they led, but they all brought a certain fortitude and a progressive attitude to their lives on isolated lighthouses.

Evelyn Richardson, Maggie Boutilier, and Madeline Lent were quite different women, living in different circumstances, but they shared a strength that is unmistakable. Richardson of course, has become well-known in lighthouse and literary circles through her writing; Lent and Boutilier are comparatively unknown, their accomplishments recognized only by their families and a thinning number of folks in their local communities.

Six decades after its original publication, Evelyn's book *We Keep A Light* remains the best and most comprehensive account of lightkeeping in Atlantic Canada. The book's staying power is a tribute to its author's ability to convey a sense of time and place through her descriptions of Bon Portage Island and her accounts of family life.

Born on nearby Stoddart's Island (known to her as Emerald Isle) in 1902, Evelyn later lived in Clark's Harbour, then Bedford, before her island roots eventually led her back to southwest Nova Scotia. In 1929, Evelyn and Morrill bought and moved to Bon Portage Island, where Morrill had been hired as lightkeeper. For the next thirty-five years they raised their children, farmed, and kept the light. Evelyn's background as a teacher, combined with a passionate interest in the natural and social world around her, led her to document the family's life on Bon Portage. The publication of *We Keep A Light* in 1945 opened the gates to more works—ranging from an historical novel, to non-fiction books about local history and wildlife.

Evelyn and Morrill Richardson.

Evelyn became actively involved in the preservation of the Old Meeting House in Barrington and she worked with the Cape Sable Historical Society for many years. When her family retired from Bon Portage in 1964, they donated their portion of the island to Acadia University, which still operates the Evelyn and Morrill Richardson Field Station in Biology at the lightstation.

But let's back up a bit, to 1945. Up to that point, no woman had written about lightkeeping and the life attached to it. *We Keep A Light* reveals much about the woman who was at various times (and sometimes all at once!) a writer, historian, environmentalist, teacher, author, lightkeeper's assistant, and a political activist of sorts. The book, while gentle in tone and evocative in imagery, pulls no punches. Evelyn did not shy away from addressing the drawbacks of island life, whether they be the occasional strife between the family and local residents over duck hunting on the island, or the apparent lack of concern from a government that didn't bother to install a radiophone on an island with no way to communicate with the mainland. (After the book came out, the Bon Portage light got its radiophone.) As her daughter Anne told me, "Mother was not complimentary to bureaucracy, let us say, and after *We Keep A Light* was written, she was visited by some superior members of the Department of Transport. They were quite *squiffy* about some of the things that she had written."

No doubt Evelyn's accounts ruffled a few feathers in Ottawa. But her writing only underscored the poor treatment of lightkeepers by an Ottawa-based bureaucracy more familiar with the placid waters of the Rideau Canal than the dangerous seas and drafty lighthouses that ruled the lives of lightkeepers.

In 2003, Saint Mary's University Masters student Fiona Marshall wrote her thesis on Evelyn Richardson and her role in local conservation and history. Marshall contends that Evelyn's "social concerns, liberal attitude and exemplary lifestyle...reveal feminist characteristics." And it does seem that Richardson broke out of the mould when it came to a very traditional way of life. In chronicling her choice of life, she also provided a refreshing change from the usual diet of dry, male-written historical accounts of lighthouses and coastal history.

We Keep A Light turned the little old wooden light on Bon Portage Island into a literary lighthouse and revealed some of the real goods on lightkeeping, without resorting to the hyperbole and embellishment common to the time. Take this description of U.S. lightkeepers, written by American author John J. Floherty in his 1942 book *Sentries of the Sea:*

> There is an eerie quality to the solitude of these isolated lights that sooner or later affects men's nerves. Stout-hearted as lions they do not know the meaning of physical fear. Their endurance in periods of stress is phenomenal. The records are filled with their heroisms and self-sacrifices when all the odds were

against them. They have stuck to their posts and kept the light burning on many occasions until the sea struck its final blow and carried away the tower and the men in it. They have faced starvation and thirst a hundred times without a whimper of complaint, and kept to their duty unflinchingly when all the laws of humanity would have excused them for having abandoned it.

I'd say this prose blows as hard as the storms that toppled those fearless lightkeepers in their towers. As an island dweller and a lightkeeper, Richardson didn't need to manufacture the romance. Along with her glorious descriptions of land and seascapes, she was equally at home describing the less-than-pleasant aspects of lightkeeping, such as the time the light broke down on a bitter winter night, forcing the family to turn the apparatus by hand.

No one could stand to turn the Light uninterruptedly in the cold draughty Lantern, so Laurie and I took alternate shifts of one hour, in which one of us turned the Light and the other helped Morrill in the kitchen, with the aid of hot coffee we kept on the stove all night. I optimistically went up for my first turn at the Light without putting on enough extra socks and my feet and legs were nearly paralyzed from the cold metal floor before Laurie came to relieve me at the end of the hour…there had been no leaving my post to dress more warmly and I found it a very long hour as the turning of the apparatus is done so slowly that it affords little exercise and is no help in keeping warm.

Cold feet and fatigue aside, Richardson loved her island home. She had a rare way of bringing the sights, smells and sounds of island life right off the page and into the reader's senses.

The flat dull-wet sand beach blurring into the cold grey fog, with the almost human shrieks of the wraith-like gulls rising above the hiss of the waves on the nearer beach and the thunder of the surf on the outer bars, presents a picture of desolation, utter and complete. But in contrast, around the bend of the Island, where the sun is breaking through the fog, a distant group of white sheep peacefully feeding in the bright grass against the blue of a thicket of spruce and the tender green of alders is perfectly reflected across the unmarked waters of the pond, and might be a pastoral scene from the heart of a farming district miles from pounding sea, and the distant sound of the bell-buoy could come from the bell of another peaceful flock beyond the mist.

Maggie and Wentie Boutilier at Croucher's Island.

Richardson's legacy—as a mother, wife, writer, historian, environmentalist and gentle activist—survives to this day in the form of her books, a school and a literary prize in her name and in Acadia University's stewardship of her beloved island.

My Island of Dreams

Evelyn Richardson embraced island life. She also took the unusual step of writing about it. Other lighthouse women were not as keen on the life, but made the best of a situation that didn't appeal to them.

Maggie Boutilier comes to my mind. I met her daughter Geraldine in 2002 when I was compiling oral history for the Nova Scotia Lighthouse Preservation Society. We talked about island life and her memories of family, but it wasn't until Geraldine hauled out her old photo albums that I really began to *see* her mother—beaming amidst her prized delphiniums, hamming it up with her eldest son, chopping wood—always *smiling*. But the smiles belied her real feelings about life on the tiny island.

For more than two decades, beginning in 1922, Maggie and her husband Wentworth (Wentie) lived on Croucher's Island in St. Margaret's Bay.

They were married in early 1918. Within a few days Wentie shipped overseas to fight with the 85th Nova Scotia Highlanders. Dug into muddy holes in the battlefield and always on the lookout for snipers, Wentie was stricken with trench leg. He spent the remainder of his tour in a military hospital, returning to Nova Scotia in May 1919.

The experience changed Wentie. Once a cheerful man who loved company and music, he became increasingly withdrawn. His daughter, Geraldine, remembered her mother saying that Wentie "went to war and came home a wrecked man."

But his status as a World War One veteran helped get him a job as the keeper of the Croucher's Island light. In late 1922 Maggie dutifully accompanied him and their two little girls to the eight-hectare (twenty-acre), spruce-covered island halfway up the bay between Black Point and French Village. She later wrote that Wentie told her they'd try island life for one year, and if it didn't work out, they'd quit.

That "one year" lasted until November 1944.

Maggie later wrote about her life on Croucher's Island. Daughter Geraldine told me she'd wanted to call the book *My Island of Dreams*. When I asked her why, she said simply, "because that's all she had. There was no hope." The book came out in 2003, seventeen years after Maggie's death, with the title *Life on Croucher's Island*.

It was a tough life for the gregarious woman who loved company and family. Geraldine says Maggie didn't leave Croucher's Island for six months after she first arrived. In the winter, ice made it impossible to make the 1.6-kilometre boat ride to Boutilier's Point. She had two-year-old Ethel and infant Geraldine (and three more kids to come!), and she had a husband who suffered "war nerves," and who sometimes couldn't do the physical work needed for island life. It was a tough go from the very start.

Maggie B. and her son Bert tussle over a slice of pie.

But from the very beginning, Maggie took a leading role in island life. Today, Geraldine has photo albums crammed with family snapshots from Croucher's—feeding the cows and hens, boat trips ashore, picnics, summer visitors, and family fun. In every picture, Maggie is beaming: as she presents a smart salute while wearing her son's air force coveralls, displaying a hooked rug, or laughing as she faces her son Bert in a mock battle for a slice of pie.

Summer was a good time for Maggie. Visits from family and fishermen, Girl Guide outings and big meals in the lighthouse were the staff of life for a woman who thought nothing of throwing together a last-minute meal for a boatload of visitors. During the war years, sailors from the convoys anchored in the bay often came to the lighthouse to play cards and sample some of Wentie's sauerkraut and Maggie's pickles and sausages.

Summer also meant time for gardening. Maggie transformed the brush- and spruce-covered area around the lighthouse into lush gardens full of delphiniums, roses, honeysuckle, and apple and pear trees. Visitors compared Maggie's gardens to the Public Gardens in Halifax. Trellises and a hammock and little nooks carved out of the scraggly spruce by Maggie brought a touch of civilization to a place that for the rest of the year presented a continual struggle for survival.

She had the right tools for the job, though. When I exclaimed over a photo of Maggie chopping wood, Geraldine said, "To be truthful, when it came to a job like that, Mother was stronger than Dad."

As son Bert wrote in a tribute after Maggie's death in 1986, "On the island, everything ran by 'Norwegian Steam.' In their twenty-two-year stay on the island, no draught animal or motorized device ever moved a pound of the tons and tons of supplies that were carried, wheeled or dragged up the steep hill to the lighthouse. But Maggie did! A robust woman, she was capable of shouldering a hundred-pound sack of stock feed and carrying it up the hill."

All the while, whether hauling supplies or making sausages or washing clothes or gardening or making clothes, Maggie was there for her children. Her biggest worry was that they receive a proper education. She had grade eight herself, but wanted her children to go farther.

Geraldine (Boutilier) Stevens.

Through correspondence, and later school on the mainland, most of her five kids got at least that far. Bert went on to join the RCMP after a few years in the air force. Wayne joined the Mounties as well, and the girls all married and had children.

Back on the island, Maggie made up for educational shortcomings by teaching her children respect for the nature surrounding them. Geraldine told me that "by being on an island, we learned a lot of things that other children wouldn't learn—gardening, and how the soil has to be manured to make the seeds grow. We grew peanuts one year as an experiment, and they grew! And even watermelons!"

Maggie also coached the girls in embroidery and quilting. Geraldine says that after a few first prize–winning entries in local exhibitions, "we were told not to *dare* put any more needle-work like that one [into competition] because it wasn't fair to the other children." Even Bert got in on the action, creating an embroidered bunny. Maggie's amused critique was, "He sure put a *reliable* backbone on that bunny! He embroidered it twice!"

Strong and supportive as she was, Maggie had her moments of weakness. She suffered debilitating headaches that left her helpless in bed. She endured Wentie's "war nerves," which made him withdraw from the joyful ruckus of the rest of the family. When it was all just a bit too much, Maggie liked to retire to the hayloft for a bit of quiet time. More often than not, it was an all-too-brief respite from a relentless work schedule, when, as Geraldine remembers, "we usually found her and cuddled up there with her." She paused, thinking back more than seventy years. "She didn't seem to mind being found."

And so passed twenty-two years of Maggie Boutilier's life. As I sat in her daughter's kitchen in Upper Tantallon, surrounded by photo albums and Maggie's hooked rugs, I was struck by all this evidence of a woman who gave up so much so that her family could be happy on Croucher's Island. Her daughter, Geraldine, delicate and soft-spoken at eighty-four and, at the same time, as sharp as a tack in outlook, paused after I asked her what she thought about all her mother's sacrifices for her family. Through a few tears she said, "What a loss she was…"

Loss, yes, but during her exile on Croucher's Island, Maggie Boutilier made the very best of a tough life, and in doing so laid a strong foundation for her own lighthouse kids.

The Most Important Light on the Island

Maggie B. and Evelyn Richardson illustrate opposite ends of the lighthouse experience. Evelyn willingly embraced the life, while Maggie B. did so for her family's sake. But what of the scores of other lighthouse women?

As I think back to my early days on Brier Island, Madeline Lent stands out as representative as many of these women, combining a

Madeline Lent helps paint the Brier Island light in the 1960s.

certain resignation to a life of isolation, with the desire to enjoy their lot as much as possible.

Born in Weymouth, Digby County, in 1924, Madeline became a high school teacher at the tender age of eighteen. When she took up a teaching job in Westport, on the last island at the end of Digby Neck, she met Donald Wickerson Lent. They fell in love and married soon after.

Wick was fishing at the time, but having a tough go of it. He'd lost a leg in a hunting accident as a young man, making life at sea doubly dangerous. When the chance came up for a job at Grand Passage Light on the island's northern tip, Madeline was all for it. "Yes!" she told Wick. "Anything to keep you off the water!"

By the time Madeline moved to the Grand Passage lighthouse on Brier Island's northern tip, things were looking up. The family had electricity. They were only a five-minute drive from a village with stores, churches and a post office. But nature soon reminded Madeline that life on the lights hadn't changed greatly in the past fifty years. As she wrote in an article for the *Digby Courier*, it was a few days after Christmas, 1960, when they faced their first "nor-easter":

> [It was] a real doozer. Gales, sleet and snow beat against the dwelling. Even the smallest dent in the insulating armor seemed to become a wind-spread rent. We moved the children, beds and all, into the kitchen, along with most of the articles from the pantry. Electricity failed during the height of the storm and Wickerson raced to the light to get a lamp going. The next morning our home looked like a rhinestone igloo outside but like a London blitz blackout within. Frozen spray covered every wall and window, keeping the sunlight out.

But nothing, it seems, could keep the sun out of Madeline's lighthouse experience. Even while she raised four kids she kept alive her interest in people, history and travel. Her daughter Faye remembered that "Mom was a realist. Although she would have loved to travel the world and visit all of the exotic places that she had read about, she knew that financially and practically it was impossible. Not one to dwell on what she could not have, she used her love of books and people to take her to all of those places she longed to visit."

She held classes in a local home, teaching English to ten members of a family fresh from Holland, as well as working in one of the village stores. She spent painstaking hours researching a book about the history of Brier Island.

All the while, lightstation and family gobbled up Madeline's time—there were four kids to raise and long days when she filled in

Madeline Lent with her grandchildren at Western Light, not long before her death. Note the rocks and sea through the window.

as an unofficial assistant to Wick, even though there were three paid keepers on the station!

Madeline kept up an active correspondence with folks around the world and delighted in news from places she knew she'd never see. After Wick died in 2005, Faye unearthed a slew of postcards from my own mother, who had sent Madeline cards during her travels in Britain and Canada in the early 1970s. Anne and Madeline had met after my folks bought a summer camp just up the road from the light. They became good friends and carried on a correspondence until Madeline died.

Visitors to the station were an added delight—the island was popular with birdwatchers before whale-watching became the big moneymaker on the island. Brier also attracted a few folks looking to get away from it all. One day in the early seventies, Madeline noticed a stranger wandering down the back shore to the lighthouse. He was, as Faye remembered, young, with "long hair, beard, knapsack, dirty and scary looking to most. Never one to scorn or look down on anyone," Madeline began to chat with the young man.

It turns out the young fellow was a well-educated artist and writer from New York. He'd been camping out on the island's back shore. Faye doesn't know if he ever revealed his reasons for "hiding out," but the artist and the lightkeeper's wife became fast friends. The young man visited the lighthouse often, where he and Madeline "spent hours talking about philosophy, art, writing, and the outside world." If he didn't show up for a few days, Madeline would take some food and walk along the shore to find him. The young man ended up coming back to the island every year, eventually buying an old workshop in the village.

In the late summer of 1976, Madeline learned she had inoperable cancer. Faye recalled the doctors telling her mother she could extend her life for a couple of years with cobalt treatments. Unfazed by the disease that would shortly claim her life, Madeline chose not to take the treatments. She died on March 3, 1978, leaving her unfinished book about Brier Island, four children, and a husband who never really got over her death.

The young artist was on the ferry that day as Madeline was rushed to hospital. He later told Faye that her death was "equivalent to seeing the most important light on the island permanently snuffed out."

5

Foghorns
THE VOICE OF CONSCIENCE

NOVA SCOTIA FOG HAS A WOOLLY QUALITY. IT steals in from the sea, insulating the coast in a thick, damp, heavy blanket. It is a dangerous cover, hiding familiar landmarks, muffling sounds, disorienting mariners.

"Thick as Aunt Maggie's quilt today," lightkeeper Reg Smith used to say when wisps of fog blew by the windows of the keeper's house on Whitehead Island in Argyle Sound, Yarmouth County.

Out at the lighthouse the little foghorn trumpet sent its warning seaward for three seconds every half minute, sometimes for days and weeks on end. Just in case there might be someone out there who might need to know that he was getting close to Whitehead Island and closer to home after a hard day hauling lobster traps.

Today, the hoots, bellows, grunts and whistles of the old Nova Scotia coast are a fading memory. Ships still use large air-powered horns as a warning and signalling device in fog, but on land, only a few low powered electronic foghorns remain from a once-extensive—and noisy!—system of aids to navigation.

Before radar and global positioning (GPS) made the coast safer and so much quieter, the foghorn was king along the Nova Scotia shoreline. Almost every lighthouse had some form of sound signal, from the lowly hand-cranked foghorn, to the clanging clockwork bell, to the

Until recently, the little electronic trumpet at the Bon Portage lighthouse sent out a warning in fog. An identical horn is still in use at Grand Passage.

mighty and deafening diaphone. All of these devices served the same purpose—to identify the station from which they were sounded, and to guide vessels past danger and into safe harbour.

Fog signals came about relatively late in the grand scheme of lighthouse history, dating to the mid-eighteenth century in Great Britain. Some keepers used cannons to warn shipping away from their lighthouses, firing shots into the fog at regular intervals. Others used bells, some of which were sounded by hand. All came to be operated by clockwork and later, gas and electric motors. Although not common in Nova Scotia, a few bells operated along our coast, even into the mid-twentieth century.

As late as 1950, duties for the keeper of the Horton Bluff light near Avonport included sounding a bell in fog. But not one of those new-fangled automatic ones! His was entirely manual, sounded at any time of the day or night in response to "Where am I?" toots from vessels travelling into Hantsport. The Horton Bluff keeper was a pragmatic fellow: A rope tied to the clapper of his bell ran through his kitchen window, where he could sit in his rocker (pipe clenched stoically in his teeth?) and tug on the rope in answer to a signal from the sea.

Even the motorized bells were labour intensive. Former Brier Island lightkeeper Wick Lent remembered when the mechanism at the Grand Passage light would break down.

"Poor old Mr. Charlie Buckman would be up there with his watch in one hand and a sledgehammer in the other," Wick said. "When it would come time he would 'BONG'. He'd watch again and 'BONG.' He done that for hours and hours by hand!"

Timing was critical. The intervals between the bongs and the bangs helped mariners identify the particular lighthouse the sound was coming from—crucial information when a change in course could either lead a boat onto the rocks or guide a mariner to safe harbour.

But fog has always been a capricious mistress and along with her cohort the wind, she often snatched the sound of a tolling bell away from the straining ears of a lost sailor to send it somewhere else where it wasn't needed. Mariners needed a powerful sound signal that could carry a great distance and, as much as possible, overcome the meddling effects of wind and water.

By the mid-nineteenth century, lighthouse authorities in England and the United States began to experiment with various types of horns operated by compressed air. Some used reeds to make noise, like blowing into a saxophone. The siren used a trumpet and a rotating disc through which compressed air blew, producing a massive, wailing sound.

Trinity House, the English lighthouse authority, installed a siren at the Lizard Lighthouse in 1878. A local newspaper reporter heard the siren blowing, saying the sound was "not so loud and disturbing as was anticipated [but] the sound is very weird and melancholy…with prolonged reverberating echoes through the surrounding precipices and caves."

This diaphone, from Lennard Island, BC, was one of the last to be removed from service in Canada. The big valve at the bottom provided the "speaking" air for the horn's massive blast.

The English and Scottish lighthouse authorities favoured the siren, using it until the 1980s, when it was replaced in most cases by auto-mated electronic horns. But it was eight decades earlier, in 1902, when

the art of high-powered fog signalling reached its zenith, with the development of the diaphone.

Originally developed as a "powerful tonal device for church organs," the diaphone came to the attention of Canadian inventor John P. Northey, who patented the invention as a foghorn. Northey forced compressed air through a slotted, reciprocating piston to produce an alarming, low-pitched blast ending with a characteristic grunt. Thus was born the most powerful foghorn ever to be developed.

Anne and Stanley Flemming's children got used to the foghorn at Chebucto Head pretty fast. They had to—it was just a few feet from their house, behind the clothesline!

The diaphone became a part of the soundtrack for coastal Europe and North America, as hundreds of horns blasted their deep-voiced warnings into the fog. A 1950s brochure from the British lighthouse manufacturers Chance Brothers stated:

> On board ship sounds have more meaning than they have on land. A sound signal has to compete with a host of other significant noises, and its usefulness depends not only upon its carrying power, but also on some quality which renders it instantly recognizable, its meaning instantly clear.

The Chance copywriter went so far as to say the diaphone "speaks through the rival clamour of machinery, wind, bells, whistles and sirens like the voice of conscience."

There's nothing like the "voice of conscience" to guide the fisherman and the sailor safely home. But for anyone who remembers that harmonic, eardrum-cracking sound terminating in a seismic grunt, it seems impossible to believe that lightkeepers and their families could maintain personal sanity while the horn was on, especially during a straight month of fog!

Strangely enough, Nova Scotia lighthouse people accepted the blast of the foghorn as part of their daily lives. During foggy days on Cape Sable, Reg Smith's mother would lay the china flat on the pantry shelves when the horn was blowing—otherwise it would end up on the floor— and then forget about the noise. I remember listening in on a keeper on Machias Seal Island, talking with a friend on the VHF radio on nearby Grand Manan. After some idle chit-chat, the keeper remarked, "Fog's rolled in. The horn just started up. I'll sleep good tonight with that blattin' bastard goin'!"

Keepers on watch said the only time they noticed the horn was when it stopped for some reason—usually sending at least one attendant flying out to the engine room to see what was wrong!

Similarly, many lighthouse kids say they'd notice the horn when Dad or Mum turned it on and, after that, no one would take any notice of the regular blasts and grunts. Reg Smith remembered one summer in the 1940s when the horn blew continuously for twenty-eight days at Cape Sable. Finally, the weather cleared and "the old man shut the horn off at two o'clock in the mornin'. There was seven kids got out of bed to see what was goin' on and to go have a look at the lights in Clark's Harbour. First time we'd seen 'em in a month!"

For generations, the foghorn was a crucial aid to navigation for mariners. Today, it has been usurped by electronic aids that silently but oh-so-accurately tell a skipper where he or she is. Some of the romance of the coast has gone as a result, along with the distinctive warning sound that a few small boats still need.

Fortunately, some of that romance lives on in the stories of the people who lived so close for so long to their noisy, warning fog signals.

THE FOGHORN WAS THE LIFESAVER

Lighthouses are oft lauded as symbols of safety for seafarers, standing resolutely against dark and tempest. What mariner would not thrill to the beam of light from a lofty tower, guiding the way to safe harbour? But fog throws a monkey wrench into this overblown, romantic image. Thick, wet and blinding, it renders lighthouses useless, no matter how powerful the light and lens.

So when the fog rolled in, the foghorn was the number one navaid for all mariners.

Ronnie Kenney began lobstering with his father Charles in the 1940s. Later, he went hand-lining off Seal Island, twenty-two kilometres west of Cape Sable, at the extreme southwest tip of Nova Scotia.

The place breeds fog, and as Ronnie told me, fishermen depended heavily on foghorns for guidance.

"Foghorns were the main thing," he said. "One hundred percent. Back then you had just a compass and a watch you had to run your time. Then you stopped and listened for a foghorn. The foghorn was the lifesaver. The old foghorns, you could hear them for miles. Many a times I've been to Seal Island and the tides were a little stronger than I expected. When I steamed my time—I'd leave Cape Island and I'd run an hour and a half—I knew I'd be gettin' close to the island. I'd always stop, listen to see if I could hear the foghorn to see if I was above or below the island. That's where you got your bearings from."

Sometimes you got your bearings from a long way away. Sid Smith, who grew up at the Cape Sable lightstation, told me how his foghorn helped save a boatload of fishermen who ran afoul of a German U-Boat.

The fishermen were sword-fishing on Georges Bank. It was August 1942, on a calm day with thick fog. The crew was ordered off their boat and into two dories. The U-boat then unceremoniously shelled the vessel, sending it to the bottom as its crew began a grueling row in what they hoped was the direction of land.

"Percy Richardson from Lockeport was the captain," Sid said, "and he later told Dad, 'We heard this foghorn blowin' and I figured it up and it had to be forty-two miles off!' There were eleven of them. I think there was three that couldn't row. One fellow had the muscle on his arm blown off and one fellow had a piece of shrapnel that went right through his wrist. One old guy had his ribs all scraped up from shrapnel."

The men spent two and a half days rowing with blistered and cracked hands, ropes linking their dories. All the while they listened to the faint blasts of the Cape Sable foghorn. Exhausted, they reached the Cape just as the weather cleared.

Sid's second cousin Reg Smith—who grew up on Cape Sable in the 1940s, and later became a keeper there—told me just how important it was to keep an eye peeled for vessel traffic.

"We were up in the garden, hoein' potatoes as a matter of fact! It was Mum and Dad and myself and the next thing I knew the old man said, 'Holy Jesus! There's the *Empress of Canada!*' It was one of those Canadian Pacific boats that used to run to Saint John from England with passengers. The fog was layin' off. This particular day I s'pose the visibility was likely four, five miles. And that ship was comin' *right* for the Cape.

"The old man threw his hoe down and he took off at a mad dash. Of course we had air up in the tanks, for the foghorn. We had a little rope lever you could salute boats with—blow the horn by hand.

"He give that thing a couple or three yanks. It was really funny, 'cause one minute the boat's comin' straight at us and next minute we saw her swing and we saw her stern goin', back out to safety."

Even the small hand-operated horns found at smaller lightstations were crucial to vessel safety. In her delightful book *B Was For Butter*, Evelyn Richardson provides a dramatic account of the importance of the little horn on Bon Portage Island, near Shag Harbour, during World War Two. Evelyn was about to take a rhubarb pie out of the oven on a calm June morning when "a foghorn's blast tore through the fog and set the windows buzzing."

Such a deep-throated bellow could not come from any of the little coastal steamers which occasionally passed the Point, and *no* ship, big or small, should be so perilously near our shore. I braced for the grinding crash of metal hull on granite rock, even as I wondered, *Can I reach our horn and send a warning in time?*

I…ran through the open back doorway…and around to the front of the lighthouse where the small hand horn sat on the narrow grassy slope between the tower and the shore. This was a box containing bellows and a reed, a trumpet-shaped horn in one end and a stick-handle on one side to pump bellows. Since the outbreak of war and the possible threat of enemy craft in our waters, the horn had been blown almost solely to answer the breathy hoot of a conch shell or the quavering note of a small boat horn, as local fishermen made their way home along our eastern shore.

Never had I pumped the handle of the little red box more prayerfully. The result was the familiar thin bleat instead of the powerful roar I would have wished, but I consoled myself, *There's no wind to whir it away; no thunder of surf to drown it. It may help. If the ship hasn't already struck.* I caught, fog diffused, but close, the heavy pulsing of engines and the churning of screws in shallow water. I gripped the handle hard and sent a second "Keep Off!" against the fog wall.

As if they had been waiting for the horn's quavering voice, the ship's propellers began to thrash mightily. In reverse. I could picture the high stern dragged downward as the blades grabbed the grey-green water and sent it curling landward, to spank the shore rocks. The engines stopped. Dead silence. Then the fog rippled, like a curtain brushed in passing, as the throb of motors resumed. The next blast of the ship's horn told me she had made a right-angle turn and was headed seaward.

I JUST LOVED THAT OLD THING!

Aside from being lifesavers for folks at sea, foghorns were a source of pride, interest and amusement to some lightkeepers. Take the case of Sidney Smith.

Lightkeeping was in Sid Smith's blood. He also loved foghorns (and still does), especially the diaphone. He and his father, Benjamin, knew every valve cover of the diesels that powered the compressors, every joint in the air pipes and every slot in the piston that produced that splendid blast and grunt.

Even when I spoke to him, Sid's face lit up when he talked about the Cape Sable diaphone. "I just loved that old thing! I suppose being a truck driver might be fun and there's a lot of people who drive trucks, but how many people operate anything that can make *that* much noise? And perhaps if you play with it a little you can get it to do a little better! I guess I learned that from my Dad because I know he loved that old diaphone.

Sid and Betty June Smith take a tea break below Cape Sable's big diaphone in the 1950s.

"The diaphone ran on two operating valves, a large one and a small one. The 'grunt' was because one operating valve had shut off but the other one still had enough air trapped in between the two valves to keep one valve open. That's where you got the 'grunt' from. So if you had more pipe between your small operating valve and your diaphone you'd get a longer grunt on the other end! 'Course Dad knew all these things because he'd been operating diaphones all his lightkeeping days. I know he was getting everything out of that poor old diaphone that it had to give! I always used to tell everybody how that seaweed down behind the engine room would all stand right on end when that thing would blow.

"They'd say, 'Oh no, it doesn't! Does it really?'"

Keeping an eye out for fog was one of Sid's—and his father's—most important duties. It meant that someone had to be awake and on watch at all times, alert for the tell-tale wisps and banks of grey, wet wool that could envelope the station for days and weeks at a time.

"The Cape Sable ledge, which was really the reason for the station being there in the first place, ran off to the sou'west of the lightstation about four miles and there was a big buoy right on the end of the ledge," he said. "When you couldn't see the buoy or the light from the buoy we usually started the fog alarm engine. You pulled on the air brake and got the engine started and then when it got up to speed you threw the compressor into gear. When the air tank got up to thirty pounds, you turned on your timing devices and this gave you seventeen seconds silence and a three second blast."

Once Sid and his father had everything running, they'd have to time their engines so the horn would blow its trademark blast and keep the air pressure at the right level. The engine room was a noisy, hot, smelly place to work (although to some the smell of diesel and warm lube oil and paint was just right), but Sid loved it. When everything was running smoothly, he could sit in the fog alarm's small office, feet up on a desk, near a large window overlooking his roaring engines.

I*T LITERALLY WAS LIKE SOMEBODY HAD COME INTO THE HOUSE!*

Maintaining a large foghorn was time-consuming, sleep depriving, and hard on the ears, to boot. The situation was doubly difficult if you worked on a rock station—where house, lighthouse and engine room were all crammed into a small space.

Jim Guptill spent more than a decade on isolated rock lighthouses, including two years on Gull Rock, off Lockeport on the South Shore. When the fog shut in there was no way to escape the deafening blasts of the horn, necessitating some creative coping skills. Jim told me what it was like, complete with pauses for blasts of the horn.

"Lightkeepers did a lot of…

"…waiting for a few moments before they…

"…finished a conversation."

During a service visit, one of the Coast Guard technicians commented to Jim that even if it was a sunny day, it was interesting to note that a lightkeeper would "rest a moment and then he'd pick up his… story and finish it off."

The pauses were just part of it. Living with all that sound was something that took getting used to. "The noise filled the *whole* building," Jim remembered. "The house, the windows, shook, the dishes rattled a bit and it was a very large, audible sound. It was huge! You stopped *whatever* you were doing and waited until it went away and then you continued on. The longest period of continuous running of the old-type foghorn was fifty-six days on Gull Rock. I was there for twenty-eight of those!

"It was no good to wear earplugs because it was a presence more than a sound. It literally was like somebody had come into the house. A very large noisy, plump somebody had taken over your life for just that five seconds!"

A hand-cranked foghorn, manufactured by Powers Brothers in Lunenburg. These little horns kept lighthouse families busy in foggy weather.

NOW WHEN WILL HE CALL?

At small harbour and island lights the hand horn was the rule rather than the exception. A simple wooden box held a bellows system and one or two copper horns, both with metal reeds that vibrated when air was pumped through them. Think of a bicycle horn with a rubber bulb, only larger.

Hand horns produced a sound commensurate with the amount of effort that went into pumping them. The trick was to work the lever vigorously enough to produce a steady tone, instead of a series of kazoo-like wheezes.

From this description, the hand horn does not sound like a particularly effective or powerful signal, but it must have been helpful for mariners. A glance through *Nova Scotia Lists of Lights, Buoys and Fog Signals* from the 1940s shows dozens of stations marked "Hand Horn—answers vessels' signals."

Jerseyman Island was one such station. Russ Latimer grew up on the little island near Arichat, where his father served as keeper for a quarter of a century. More than sixty years after leaving the island, Russ described the hand horn for me.

"The horn was a double reed box affair, with a lever-type handle, and you sat on it by straddling it. You pumped the lever to and from you. It gave quite a blast! It was a rather nice musical sound. Those reeds were removable if for any reason they became clogged up with snow or ice, or damaged."

In thick weather, the whole family took part in horn blowing. For the kids, the reward was usually a special dessert. And for Russ, there was the anticipation of that commanding whistle blast through the fog.

"I hardly remember a ship coming in there that we weren't really expecting or a ship that we didn't know about," he said. "We had the steamship company in Sydney known as W. N. MacDonald. In my time he operated the Canso-Arichat-Mulgrave run.

"They were beautiful ships—clipper bow steam yachts. Then the freight boats were operated; C. J. Hendry of Halifax operated the *Dominion Shipper* and *Dominion Coaster*. Then there were fishing smacks—the *Seldom In* and the *Josephine K.*

"In spring there was a lot of fog. In winter it was snow and heavy rain. We always had a mark across the other side of the channel which gave us an indication when we should stand by the horn or when some-body would be calling."

You couldn't always hear a ship from inside the lighthouse, so when the fog or snow shut in, someone had to stand watch outside, usually just inside the boathouse. The first long blast of a horn or whistle would send Russ scurrying to the shore to pump out a reply.

"We wouldn't spend a long time at the horn," he noted. "Probably no more than an hour unless the ship was having trouble finding the channel through soundings and listening to the breakers on the shore. They knew every crop of rocks, as we did. You pretty well felt your way in.

"Once he passed the lighthouse he never asked for you to blow a blast from astern. The skippers often used to say, 'We hear you blowing. When we blow the international signal for fog, we're not asking you for a reply on the horn.' So we never answered their signals if we knew we were astern of them."

WAITING FOR A FOGHORN TO BLOW!

Melda and Marie Palmer remember their own foghorn duties with less enthusiasm. The girls grew up at Owl's Head lighthouse on the eastern shore during the 1930s and '40s. Melda, rough in voice and matter-of-fact in manner, wryly explained her summer foghorn duties.

"Marie and I, we used to spend our summer vacations out on a rock, waitin' for a foghorn to blow! We used to have to blow the old horn to bring the fishermen in."

The drill didn't impress Melda.

"*That* was our summer vacation!" she said, snorting. "We had all kinds of fog. It was horrible! It used to be fine up in the village but the fog would bank out to sea. So we were out there every day, 'cause there were fishermen out there every day. Then there were the supply ships that used to supply the stores. There were no trucks then. And there was the O.K. Service boats that came from Boston to pick up the lobsters from the wharf. We used to guide them in once a week."

In these days of legal responsibility, liability and due diligence, it's almost impossible to fathom that two young girls, not even in their teens, were tasked with guiding all manner of vessels into Owl's Head Harbour. Although the girls didn't relish the job, Marie was aware of the importance of her task, perched on a rock in a blinding fog, pumping away for hours on end.

"The boats would answer us back, and then you'd see them goin' by. They'd be close enough to the edge of that cliff you could see them. We pretty much knew who all the fishermen were and you'd know when the last one was in."

FUN WITH FOGHORNS

A foghorn—even a little wooden box cranked by a child—is not a toy. For folks such as Sid Smith, the foghorn was a piece of complex machinery that afforded him pleasure in its operation and upkeep. But for other keepers and their children, foghorns were occasionally a source of amusement—especially when tourists were around.

Don Gallagher's father Edward kept watch at the Chebucto Head light for twenty-two years, starting in 1928. One of his most important duties was to tend the foghorn, located at the bottom of a steep cliff below the lighthouse. Don told me that once in a while, curious visitors would pick their way down the hill for a little taste of lighthouse life. Sometimes they got more than they bargained for.

"You didn't stand around underneath the horn when it blew," he said, grimacing. "It had an 'AAAAHH' at the end of it. Like a 'BOOOO-AAAAH.'"

Don's father liked to have a bit of fun with the BOOO-AHHHH. When visitors came down to the fog alarm, they'd be ushered into the building, with its thundering diesels and flapping belts. It was too noisy to talk, so Edward would lead folks outside, where it was quieter. For a while.

Don took up the story. "You could just hear the drone of the engines outside. Dad would close the door behind him and all of a sudden that horn would let go! If you'd had a barber around you could have given everybody a perfect brush cut because their hair was standing right on end! Right underneath the horn and he'd just grin. It was funny! I guess we were all immune to it to a degree. Dad had a sixth sense when it was going to happen. I think it blew twice every sixty seconds and he knew just when that thing was gonna go off. He had it down pat!"

A large Type F diaphone (sizes ranged from the petite Type A to the gargantuan Type L, with a range of seven to ten nautical miles) graced the Brier Island lightstation until 1971, when the Coast Guard replaced it with a stack of high-pitched electronic emitters.

But in the 1960s, the old diaphone was still a going concern, much to the appreciation of local fisherman and to the chagrin of unsuspecting visitors. Former lightkeeper Wick Lent recalled the Brier Island horn's impact.

"Oh my God! It was one of the most powerful horns on the coast. The only ones anywheres near it were Sambro and Louisbourg lights. They were about on a par. It was so loud that when it would blow, the dishes on the shelf in the pantry in the duplex would shake. They claimed they could hear it certain times right over to Eastport, Maine. That's seventy-odd miles!"

One year the head lightkeeper's son was being married in the living room at the lightstation. Just as they were getting started, Wick looked out and saw the fog shutting in. "Uh-oh. This [is] going to be interesting," he thought as he ran for the foghorn building to start up the compressors.

"It took a while for poor old Mr. Derby the Christian Church minister to catch on," Wick remembered. "He'd say a few words and he'd watch his watch. After the fog whistle would blow then he'd say a little bit more. She had a two-and-a-half second blast and two minutes' silence and a two-and-a-half second blast. He had to work his service in through all that, till he got them married!"

Brier Island's foghorn also provided entertainment for Wick and unsuspecting visitors to the lightstation. "There was no gate at the lightstation then. You could drive right up to the foghorn and park right down under the horn. There was a big puddle there. One day this old lady and her granddaughter got out of the car and she says, 'Could we come in and see what's going on?' I said, 'Help yourselves, but it's kind of noisy!'

"So they come [inside]. In between the blasts I explained to her about the horn and showed her when the cam came around and pressed down on [the lever], that's when the noise would come. The little girl said to the old lady, 'Now watch when that thing [the timing mechanism] comes around. When that comes down it's going to make an awful noise!'" They were standing by an open window, just below the horn's massive trumpet. Wick continued:

"Then that old thing cut loose. The roar would just fairly shiver your timbers! The old lady got right down on her knees on the floor and the little girl was laughing to kill herself! The next time it blew the old lady was out in front and the little girl said 'Let it go again, let it go again!'"

Wick continued with a sly smile. "There was some odd ones. I should have recorded all of them. There was one car used to come with a young fellow and he always brought a bunch of girls. He'd always park in the same place. He knew where to park! He'd time it from along the road and just when they'd get out of the car the whistle would cut loose. The girls would go into hysterics and when they'd all get through with screaming he'd look up at me and laugh! Then he'd say, 'See you next week. The only thing different will be the crew!'"

The boom and grunt of the diaphone is now just a memory. You might hear it on TV commercials and in old movies. The few dozen horns remaining in Nova Scotia are mostly high-pitched, low-power electronic models that automatically send a "peep" into the fog.

WHO'S LISTENING, ANYWAY?

Most (if not all) fishermen now have access to radar, GPS, and plotters, and many don't spare a thought for the foghorn.

When Ronnie Kenney started fishing off Cape Sable Island six decades ago, foghorns were more important than lighthouses…period. He told me that "one time on Seal Island in the summer it was thick fog. The foghorn blowed three straight months! Never stopped! We used drail [troll] off the Elbow [about two kilometres south of Seal Island] and we'd stay off there pretty well till we figured we'd get in to the wharf just before dark. We'd have to *listen* to the foghorn to guide us up by the island."

Ronnie bought his first radar in the early 1970s. He says it wasn't long before others followed suit. When you had electronic eyes to see buoys, boats and—hallelujah!—land, there was no need to stop and listen for a faint blast to find out where you were. Now, in the twenty-first century, a plotter and a GPS unit can take any boat just about anywhere in the world without a worry. Ronnie Kenney's son Charles still fishes around Seal Island. But for him, getting there is a far cry from the days of dead reckoning.

"He's got his plotter set and when he gets to Race Point the boat stops," Ronnie told me. "She won't go no farther! They got rigs today

The Coast Guard replaced many powerful diaphones with Stone-Chance electronic horns in the early 1970s. Today's thumping car stereos have more power than these horns.

Even these modern horns (on small tower at right), operated by battery and controlled by fog detectors, are being phased out.

that it's like drivin' on a highway! You leave the wharf and turn on your computers and there's your boat just like goin' down a road. Takes you right where you're goin'!"

Ronnie told me that some folks still need foghorns—especially those who use small open boats to rake Irish moss around the islands of southwestern Nova Scotia. But there's a question as to how useful those

Lightkeeper Peter Coletti stands beside the big two-thousand-watt electric foghorn at Gannet Rock.

horns are. In the early 1970s, the Coast Guard replaced all the powerful foghorns with weaker, electronic signals that just don't have the same carrying power.

In September 1971, the venerable diaphone at the Brier Island lightstation gave a final blast, regretfully saluting its replacement—a tiny array of speakers with less power than many of today's thumping car stereos. A few folks from the nearby village of Westport came down to hear the new horn, and one wry listener noted that the new signal sounded like "an elephant in distress." Up at our summer cottage, my mother added that the new horn had a "multi-toned 'peeeroo' as opposed to the lovely old mellow 'boo-um.' We'll miss the old compressed air whistle," she wrote in the camp log that day.

The set-up certainly didn't impress lightkeeper Wick Lent: "They were useless," he told me, shaking his head. "Look, I stood with one of the guys from Ottawa right up by the lighthouse. The trawl boats from

Freeport over on Long Island were coming in and you could hear the men talking. They couldn't hear that horn. 'Where is the damn thing?,' they said. 'We can't hear the damn thing!' Those horns were useless!"

More than three decades have passed since the Coast Guard replaced Wick's old diaphone with new, "useless" emitters. Now, even those horns have outlived their purpose. Around Nova Scotia a few more horns are taken out of service each year. There's even talk that the Coast Guard will get rid of bell and whistle buoys. The coast may one day soon be silent. No more "voice of conscience" for mariners and fishermen. No need to shut engines down, ears straining for that faint but unmistakable sound. No "blattin' bastard" to lull its keepers to sleep.

Just the wind, waves, and thick, wet, woolly fog.

6

Wind, Waves, and Weather Whims

Once, while I was a lightkeeper on Gannet Rock in the Bay of Fundy, a local fisherman called the lighthouse to ask about weather conditions. It was a snotty winter night, blowing thirty-five to forty knots from the northeast and cold, with spray lashing at the lighthouse windows.

As I stood at the marine radio near the old oil heater in the living room, we talked about how miserable it was and how exposed Gannet Rock was—this half-acre, wave-pounded rock fourteen kilometres south of Grand Manan. "Wouldn't catch me dead out there," said the fisherman. "Nowhere to run when the weather's bad!"

Now, this guy was a scallop fisherman—a dirty, rough job that would often take him, in

Gull Rock, Nova Scotia, in snotty winter weather.

the middle of winter, into the freezing jaws of the bay, working thirty-six or more hours at a stretch on the deck of a pitching, spray-drenched, wave-tossed boat.

Nope, I thought. Give me this forsaken rock any day. At least it can't sink!

During my time as a lightkeeper on Gannet Rock, I came as close to being on a boat as I could on an immovable piece of land. In the early 1990s I recorded these observations in my diary:

> In some ways this place is like a ship, with the lantern as the bridge and the tower and house as the superstructure and afterdeck, respectively. The continuous rumble of the diesels, the traffic on the VHF radios and the endless swell rolling by creates the illusion that the rock is moving slowly and steadily over the sea. The smells of cigarettes, diesel fuel and cooking add to the deception.

> In a stiff easterly it was quite disconcerting to sit in the living room and suddenly catch a wave that would hit the seawall just outside, SMASH!—sending spray slashing into the window and then running, foaming, down the glass.

Even bolted and cemented and hammered into Gannet Rock as we were, the old station did have some motion. When the forecast called for winds in excess of forty knots, we'd tie down anything that might want to take flight, close up the shutters on the old house, and settle down in front of the TV. If it was a real bad breeze—say a sou'wester, blowing storm to hurricane force—I'd get restless and climb the tower. The higher you got, the more it shook. If you put your back against the wall, you could feel the 160-year-old timbers shiver and surge as the wind slammed into it. It put you in mind of being on a pitching schooner in the teeth of a gale.

Lightkeepers, like fishermen, were often at the mercy of the sea. Especially in the early days, before reinforced concrete towers and sturdy houses gave some measure of protection against the elements. Right until the end of lightkeeping in the Maritimes, weather affected almost everything keepers did—from painting their towers and homes, to getting ashore for groceries. Weeks of blinding fog could hold you prisoner in a world defined only by the sonorous blasts of a foghorn. Monster swells and howling winds had the same stultifying effect, but added another dangerous variable— damage to buildings and danger to life.

In the fall of 1870 a whopper of a storm hit the Egg Island lightstation, about seventy kilometres east of Halifax. Massive seas slammed into the keeper's house, sending the terrified lightkeeper and his family running for the safety of the lighthouse. As they huddled inside the wooden tower, the seas made a clean sweep across their tiny, treeless island, moving their home and its contents more than forty metres away from its foundation. Successive swells tore up thirty metres of slipway and washed away all other outbuildings, boats, and the station's freshwater tank. It took the Department of Marine and Fisheries more than two years to repair all the damage.

In the early 1890s, a winter storm met the Munroe family head-on as they cowered in the lighthouse on Three Top Island, near White Head. Lightkeeper W. L. Munroe later wrote this account in a letter to the *Eastern Graphic*, a Guysborough newspaper.

> The sea in one of its fierce rushes bursted our door at ten
> o'clock at night and flooded our floors to a depth of six inches
> of water. My wife and the children scream[ed], thinking they
> were doomed. I got them gathered to a window, there to make
> our exit and flee to one of the highest peaks, but in this case
> Providence favoured us by the gale moderating and the sea
> falling some and did not cause us to face such an ordeal in a
> winter's hurricane on a naked cliff.

Three decades later and just a shade to the east at White Head Island, lightkeeper Almon Munroe barely escaped with his life when the sea decided to tear the station's fog alarm building from the granite to which it was bolted. Before this happened, Munroe spent some anxious moments trapped inside the building near the door "because the sea held [the door]," as his daughter Mary-Ellen later reported. The keeper

The bridge between the lighthouse and foghorn building at White Head Island in Guysborough County.

waited for the sea to subside a little, then ran like the dickens across the bridge to the lighthouse where his family waited. "The next morning," Mary-Ellen wrote, "there was nothing left; tanks and motors were gone. [Only] the rock was left standing."

The lightkeeper's young daughter had no romantic illusions about the sea, although in later years she described its power rather poetically in her memoir, "The Lighthouse: One of the Seven Wonders of My World." "The island was almost surrounded by high rocks," she wrote, "except for a short space where the land and the sea were almost level on the south side of the lighthouse. The sea washed lazily over these rocks in a friendly fashion, whereas the big rocks had an unfriendly attitude towards the ocean. Some times the roaring of the sea would be so loud we would have to go inside to talk."

It was almost impossible to have a conversation inside the engine room on the southern end of Gannet Rock, in the middle of the Bay of Fundy. That's where young Kay (Wilson) Ingersoll found herself in the middle of a stormy night in the 1940s. It was windy enough that her father Donald had called the Marine Agent in Saint John to ask permission to shut down the light. As the old wooden tower swayed in the buffeting gusts, mercury from the lens's rotating mechanism began to spill from its trough. Donald Wilson decided it was time to move.

Amidst slashing spray and wind, Kay and her family made a dash into the fortress-like fog signal building. Kay told me her mother made "me up a bed on a workbench. She had a huge kettle of soup. I don't know where *that* came from! There was a stove in the whistle house, so we were warm and comfortable out there. 'Course, the whistle was going because it was a storm! So that was not a very nice experience. We stayed there till the storm was over."

A hurricane that hit the Parrsboro lighthouse in the 1950s left the tower leaning like a drunken sailor.

Even lightkeepers at so-called "downtown" lights sometimes came face-to-face with the fury of the sea. In the 1950s a doozie of a storm hit the Parrsboro area. The community's lighthouse sat at the end of a breakwater in the harbour. Lightkeeper Russell Spencer was alone at the station, his wife and children ashore.

Spencer's daughter Alice Breau recalled that a man living near the mainland end of the breakwater offered to pick her father up in his boat, but Russell said, "No, I'll stay put." As he huddled in the house adjacent to the light tower, Spencer became aware that his lighthouse had developed a list. He ran up the tower to extinguish the kerosene-burning light, and then retreated to his home to wait out the blow. When the winds dropped out, the lighthouse was barely standing, leaning like a drunken sailor. The sea had undermined the old wooden tower's foundation and only two or three iron rods in the base had saved the whole thing from toppling over.

It was an extreme example of the dangers faced by lightkeepers. But for Russell Spencer, it was all in a day's work. As Alice later said, "Nothing bothered him! He'd say, 'No big thing!' He went up in that leaning tower and put the light out and came back down again. He had nerves of steel, that one!"

AT THAT VERY MOMENT, A GREEN WAVE WENT BY THE WINDOW

If you look in almost any poster shop or framing outlet, you can see Jean Guichard's famous photo of a French lightkeeper standing in the doorway of his monolithic stone tower, as a massive, foaming wave wraps itself around the base of the tower…ready to rip the keeper from his post and send him into oblivion. It is a startling image, symbolizing just how close some lightkeepers live to the elements. (Incidentally, although the photo doesn't show it, the keeper closes the door just before the wave engulfs the base of the tower.)

Canada doesn't have any grand, stone towers rising out of the sea. But we do have plenty of lighthouses where keepers have come face-to-face—literally—with the power of the ocean. Jim Guptill, for example, spent ten years on a barren patch of rock, called the Salvages, near Port LaTour in southwest Nova Scotia. It's a pretty grim spot—just a low spread of granite ledge and beach rock barely above sea level. Jim and his shift partner spent twenty-eight days at a stretch in what was essentially a concrete bunker with a light on top, a foghorn on the seaward side, and a wooden house scabbed on to one end.

For Jim, the Salvages provided a front-row seat for nature's frequent assaults on the province's coast. His eyes widened as he described to me being battered by the Atlantic.

"When you left the dwelling and entered the basement of the structure it put you in mind of a ship. In the ground floor level they had glass portholes. The glass on the things was an inch and a half or two inches thick! You could look out almost any area out of this basement in bad weather and be looking *right* into the sea. Literally! It was fascinating. It scared the living daylights out of me, but I couldn't help looking! It was like watching somebody get hit on the highway with a car! I'd get in one of these portholes and set there and say, 'Holy crap, this one's gonna be *it!*'

Then the wave would SMACK! against the side of the house. It was a crazy experience!"

With images of foaming green combers and no place to run, I asked Jim how he dealt with the constant threat of bad weather out there. He glanced upwards and smiled.

"That was best exemplified by looking at one's prayer life, because when you'd see a fall storm coming—something starting up the Carolinas—you'd start watching it. As it got closer you'd start thinking 'Oh, this is gonna be a dilly,' and you'd start praying to whatever deity it is that you worshipped. 'Listen, if you don't mind it would be marvellous if this would hit me on the low tide!' If it hit on the high tide, you were diddled! Or at least you were gonna put in a pretty rugged six or seven hours."

Jim's first experience with rough weather on the Salvages didn't last that long though. In fact, it was all over in the blink of an eye. "The first day that I was on the Salvages after moving from Gull Rock—that would be probably in April of '77—I was standing looking out the kitchen window looking over at Cape Negro and thinkin', 'Well, I haven't improved my circumstances much, except I'm getting more money now!'

"At that very moment a green wave went by the window. It went around the corner and took out the whole section that separated me from the boatshed, and left. The walkway, hundreds of tons of gravel, the whole thing right down to bedrock was just gone," Jim told me. "All of the shingles underneath of the kitchen window and around the north end of the house were all stripped off. And this was after the bad winter weather was over and done with!"

Jim said he was particularly thankful that he wasn't outside when the rogue wave hit, especially as it was his custom to jog along the walkway at midnight, when he was off duty. You couldn't let your guard down for a moment.

A gull's eye view of the Salvages, showing the walkway that was washed away by a freak wave in 1977.

"Every year you hear of somebody being washed over the side," he said, "either at Chebucto Head or out at Peggy's Cove, and there's signs up everywhere: 'Stay back from the sea. Stay Back!' Well, we were *in* that," he said. We were where people aren't allowed to walk when you're out at Peggy's Cove. So, you stayed very close to the building. When I jogged back and forth on the walkway between the house and the boathouse, I made sure that the tide was down and the weather forecast was good before I set out!"

YOU'D WASH RIGHT OUT TO SEA

For Wick Lent, it was more a question of waiting for a lull in the seas so he could run for home. On the afternoon of February 2, 1976, Wick found himself marooned in the tiny cinder block engine room at the Brier Island lighthouse.

For hours, a hundred-knot wind had whipped the Bay of Fundy into a frenzy of white water and crashing swells. The Groundhog Day storm, as it became known, hammered southwestern Nova Scotia for the better part of that day, causing hundred of thousands of dollars in damage to coastal communities. Westport on Brier Island was hit particularly hard, with many of the village's waterfront wharves and buildings—including the main general store—torn apart by extreme tides and mountainous seas.

On the western end of the island, the hundred-metre walk from the engine room to the big duplex where Wick's wife Madeline waited anxiously was normally a two-minute jaunt—even for Wick, who moved about jerkily on his prosthetic leg.

On this day, the valley between the fog alarm and the keeper's house filled with surging water again and again. It was useless for Wick to even think about leaving the building. "You'd wash right out to sea," he told me. But after about three hours Wick sensed a bit of a lull in the breakers sweeping across his lawn: "I took to my scrapers. I couldn't move too fast with an artificial leg, but I got down. When I was right abreast of the house, I looked down the shore and here's this huge great wooden box comin' at me, bouncing this way and that. It was a big crate affair, big enough to be part of a building. I lined it up and I said if that doesn't hit something pretty doggone quick it's gonna smash into the house!"

Wick rapped on the window and told his wife, Madeline, to stay inside and to watch for the box. If it looked like it was going to hit, he said, "run out the back door and stay low against the back of the house." But the wind had other plans for the box. "Across the road, there was a hill. When the box it hit that it bounced again and missed the house by about six feet. It kept right on a-goin'.

"Far as I know it's still goin'!"

IT WAS A BAD BREEZE

That same day and thirty-four kilometres to the northwest, the two lightkeepers on tiny Gannet Rock were having a decidedly worse time of it. Don Denton and Ashton Fleet had watched the weather apprehensively in the morning, as the wind worked its way from the southeast to the west, where it proceeded to whip the sea into a seething, pounding force that sent green water smashing into the keeper's house and fog-horn building.

There was nowhere to run on a rock so small you could walk around the lightstation in less than a minute. Hammering gusts buried the needle at 120 knots (221 kilometres per hour), which was as high as the numbers went on the gauge. At the height of the storm, Denton figured the wind was blowing at 130 knots (239 kph).

A westerly swell piles into Gannet Rock.

Before the seas got really bad, Denton looked out the kitchen window. Someone had left a hammer on the concrete deck outside. By this time the wind was screeching at a stiff ninety knots (166 kph), and the hammer was "blowing along the deck like a feather."

As the winds increased, they drove the sea into a fury, filling the exhaust pipes for the generators, killing the station's power supply. Don and his assistant climbed the groaning wooden tower, deafened by the wind that pummelled the 145-year-old structure. From the top, they couldn't even see the deck surrounding the station—only a frothing dirty white mass of sea and debris.

The crisis came when the sea decided to enter the house. The keepers had shuttered all windows but two. These were protected by a tall section of thick concrete seawall, and no one ever thought the sea would broach that. But it did.

The old wood-framed windows gave way before tons of water which flooded the bottom story of the house, leaving Don and Ashton to wade through cold salty water up to their knees. With the generators down and both stoves out, the men could only sit and watch what would likely be the end of Gannet Rock and its guardians.

Don's wife, Isabel, waited ashore with no idea of her husband's fate. In a *Maclean's* interview, she later said, "Some of the fishermen said Gannet Rock wouldn't be there when the storm was over. Hearing those rumours didn't help."

By nightfall the wind began to veer further to the north, opposing the monstrous seas. When I spoke with Don in the early 1990s (I had telephoned him from Gannet, where I was in the middle of a twenty-eight-day tour of duty on a calm summer day) he told me if the wind had not changed direction, they would not have seen the night through.

Finally, as a strong northwest wind beat the seas into submission, a friend on a nearby island called Don's wife, holding his CB radio to the telephone. Don was okay and Gannet Rock had survived the onslaught. As Don later told *Maclean's* reporter David Folster, "I think we possibly saw that day as rough a sea as anybody ever saw and lived to tell about it."

IT GETS KINDA HAIRY!

Across the bay, near Fundy's "wicked elbow," the lightkeepers on Cape Sable had more room to escape the sea as they were occasionally forced to do when high winds and tides flooded the sandy, grassy islet. Reg Smith remembered heading for the safety and relative comfort of the engine room during a bad blow in the 1950s.

"You gotta understand the southern end of Cape Sable is three feet below sea level to start with," he explained, "and when you get tides runnin' four feet above normal and a sea behind 'em, it gets kinda hairy! You didn't wait around 'till it started blowin' fifty miles an hour and then say, 'Well, maybe we better close the barn door!' So, we had a little bit of warning that this thing was comin' in our general direction, and when the cellar got full, the old man said, 'Well, I guess we better get outta here.'"

With the help of a safety line, the family waded out to the fog alarm building. "We were out in the engine room with a Vivian diesel bangin' away like crazy," Reg told me. "For a while it was three or four kids bawlin' and howlin', 'cause it was blowin' hard. Every now and then you'd hear the sea roll some rocks against the back of the building, but if you didn't look out the window it wasn't that bad! It was all heavy beams inside. Man! You couldn't have found any safer spot to be in!"

The Smiths spent a dry but deafening seventy-two hours in the engine room. "We took the bread and milk out to the engine room," Reg told me. "I pushed the tools aside on the workbench and put a pillow on the vice and that was my bed, next to the engine. The old man had built an office in the building, so Mum and the smaller kids went there to sleep."

Reg paused, searching for the right words to describe the family's eating arrangements during their engine room exile. "Mum was very… imaginative…about her cookin'. I think there was five or six of us kids at that time. There was no toast. Forget that! But there was oatmeal, if the engine manifold got hot enough to heat the water up! We ate oatmeal and Kraft Dinner for three days, as far as meals go. And it was all cooked on the manifold of the engine. Talk about your half-baked meals!"

Flooding was not quite the same on lofty Saint Paul Island, nineteen kilometres off the desolate northern tip of Cape Breton. But even though the northeast light was perched on a small and barren islet, a full twenty-seven metres above the sea, salt water was often an unwanted houseguest. Adalene McSheffery smiled dryly as she remembered the force of winter weather.

Adalene McSheffery with a painting of desolate Saint Paul Northeast light, where "you'd wonder where you were gonna wake up with the wind blowin' against the house!"

"Sometimes you'd go to bed at night and know you were on the island but you'd wonder where you were gonna wake up in the morning, with the wind blowin' against the house," she told me. "We had a family on there one time. They had their Christmas tree sittin' in the corner of their living room. They heard an awful racket in the night and when they got up to see what happened, the sea had hit against the house and knocked the tree over!

"The waves would break against the rocks and the wind would blow the seas right over the house. In the winter time we used to put a rope up from the houses up to the beacon room so you could get up. Many's the times I've gone up on my hands and knees, 'cause you didn't dare stand up. It'd be icy and the wind'd blow you over the cliff!"

Lightstation buildings also stood at the mercy of the wind. On Jerseyman Island in Arichat Harbour, the little lighthouse marking the entrance to Crid Pass was tied down against this possibility. Russ Latimer grew up in the tiny 8.5 metre–tall lighthouse with its attached (and drafty!) dwelling, and he told me just how breezy the place was.

"The wind blew particularly heavy at that station. It funnelled down the Strait of Canso and then veered into Crid Pass, which was the channel. Because the tower part was tapered, the wallpaper had a habit of leaving the wall and then flapping in the wind, so it was a pretty breezy place to live. When we first arrived at the lighthouse in 1930, we wondered why there were huge stays on either side of the tower—two on the west, two on the east. They were about an inch in diameter! Then the first shrieker came down the strait that winter, and we noticed how tight those shrouds were on one side and how slack they were on the leeward side! They even swayed a little bit. So they must have kept the lighthouse from toppling over!"

YOU WANNA TALK ABOUT PEOPLE RUNNING AROUND IN POLKA-DOT NIGHTGOWNS!

No matter what the time of year, the weather presented daily challenges for keepers and their families. Don Gallagher grew up on the wind-blasted granite mound of Chebucto Head, at the southern approaches to Halifax Harbour. The lighthouse sat on top of a thirty-metre cliff, making trips outside bracing at the best of times and downright dangerous in a big blow. It was often a tough go inside the house—which had the light mounted on the roof—as well. Don told me about the night the chimney blew down.

"We burned coal and wood and coke in the furnace. When they put it in the light they found that the soot was smoking up the glass on the lantern. So they built more on to the chimney. It was an awesome thing, like the Nova Scotia Power chimneys in Tuft's Cove! Poor old Santa Claus even had trouble with it.

"Anyway, the chimney blew over one night. You want to talk about people running around in polka-dot nightgowns! That was some racket! It sounded like some kind of a continuous thunderclap. What a mess! And then the house filled with smoke! Everything backed up. Oh, what a mess!"

A vigorous breeze also led to an amusing incident one drafty night at the Chebucto Head light. "Dad and his assistant used to take the old wooden storm windows off in the summer. But one of the windows didn't come off. So they left it on. We had this vicious storm. The wind was blowing, oh it was howling! And the window came off. When it did, the inside window fell down. Then the catch let go on the window blind and the blind was going BBRRRRR, around in circles. My younger brother woke up hollering like an idiot, hollering, 'Mum, come in quick, the side's out of the house!' He thought it was tarred paper between the shingles flapping!"

SHE GOT OVER IT IN TIME

Salt water: It battered lighthouses, flooded engine rooms and sent families scurrying for safety. Sometimes it came a step closer, threatening to steal family members from dry land.

Ingram and Lynne Wolfe moved to West Ironbound Island, at the mouth of the LaHave River, in the early 1960s. They had a comfortable frame dwelling with a light on top, overlooking the open Atlantic. Still, it was a challenging spot to bring up two young children, caught between a cliff edge and the deep blue sea.

Ingram himself just about lost his life when his small boat flipped one day, sending him into the frigid water. It was March and blowing "about sixty-five mile an hour," forcing Ingram to struggle to shore. "I had some problems after that, with my heart," he told me, "'cause the doctor said that I had strained the muscles of my heart from struggling in the cold water. I was lucky to survive it, really."

Not too many years later, the ocean almost claimed the Wolfes' daughter Heather. Ingram matter-of-factly described what must have been a horrendous experience for the little girl.

"My oldest daughter was washed out to sea in a heavy groundswell after a hurricane. There was one big wave hit and brought her back on the shore again. It was a very tricky place. You had to be very careful around the shore out there."

The strain of that event showed more on Lynne's face, as she filled in the details. "Heather's cousin caught her by the boot," she said, "but her boot came off and they lost her again. The next time she grabbed Heather by her hair and saved her by her long hair. Oh, it was *terrible*! It was just awful. Heather was scared of the water after that and she didn't want to go in the boat and she didn't want to go outdoors. She got over it in time, but it was a bad experience."

Similarly, a narrow escape for Kelly (Fairservice) Brown left her with respect for the sea that bordered her playground on Sambro Island, at the entrance to Halifax Harbour. Five-year-old Kelly and her older brother Phillip were playing on the granite rocks on a sunny day in the late 1960s, "calling the water names. Then, a wave just came and took us both," Kelly told me. "That was my first time ever thinking that I could die. I got wedged underneath a rock. Looking up I could just see the pool of water and the sky.

"I thought then that I was gonna die. But then another big wave come in drove me up on the beach." Less worried about the sea than facing their father, Kelly remembered that her brother, Phillip, "just kept sayin', 'Don't tell Dad, 'cause we'll be in trouble!'"

ICE

For the more northerly stations, there was another variable that made life interesting and sometime dangerous. Ice ruled the lives of the Latimer family for at least three months of the year, as it formed around their Jerseyman Island home. As Russ Latimer remembered, the ice didn't always cause the family hardship—in fact it often made it easier to get ashore, on foot.

Latimer recalled the winter of 1935 as being particularly cold, much to the delight of local residents. "I'm sure all of the population of Arichat was out enjoyin' the harbour skating, ice-boating, sleigh riding," he told me, "when this great terrible ugly old ship, smoke belching out of it, came to the edge of the ice. Everybody laughed at her, but they put a crew ashore after they closed it in against the ice edge. The crew fanned out and asked all the people to leave."

Ice at Cape Breton's Scatarie Island sometimes kept lightkeepers captive during the winter months.

It took about an hour and a half to convince people to get off the ice, most shaking their heads with disbelief that this old steamer, the *Mikula*, could bust through eighteen inches of solid ice.

Russ continued the story. "In came *Mikula* at about anywhere from five to six knots. She just hammered the hell out of the harbour. She came in the western entrance and down to the government wharf and made a few circles, to churn it all into slush so the daily boat could manoeuvre, and then she turned around and came out the western entrance where we lived.

"The next morning there wasn't one speck of ice in the harbour. Just like summer!"

During warmer winters, the ice didn't harden as well, making the trip from the lighthouse to Arichat more risky. Russ and his father would alternately row their double-ender through the slushy patches, and then climb out on the solid pans—locally called "clampers"—to push the boat to the next patch of slush or open water. Irving Latimer also built a sleigh capable of supporting the boat for longer trips over the ice.

As a teenager, Russ had a few tense moments, when one day the tide carried him into the open bay. It was all part of island life though, and harder on Dorothy Latimer than anyone else, as Russ laughingly remembered. "My poor mother! She had some worryin' to do on that place!"

A big worry for Irving Latimer was running out of tobacco in the dead of winter. Ice notwithstanding, it meant a trip to Arichat, and even Dorothy couldn't keep her husband from the perils of the ice-filled, three-quarter-mile trip to the village, as Russ told me. "'Yes, let him go,' she'd say, 'because you can't live on the same island when he's out of tobacco!'"

I SET OUTDOORS AND WATCHED 'ER BURN

Storms, wind, monster seas, and ice were just a few of the challenges faced by lightkeepers and their families. Danger from the heavens was another issue altogether. Lightning strikes were a very real threat to the legions of modest wooden towers dotting the Nova Scotia coastline.

The original tower on East Ironbound Island, off Chester, burned to the ground in January 1870 after being hit by lightning. Even the massive wood-sheathed stone tower at Shelburne's Cape Roseway light was no match for a bolt from above. In 1959 the tower was gutted after being struck, and the Department of Transport replaced the 171-year-old edifice with a concrete structure that still stands today.

It was one thing to lose a lighthouse to lightning. It was another kettle of fish entirely to be *inside* the structure during a hit. That's what happened to fifteen-year-old Ronald Spinney. Ron lived with his folks, William and Bertha, on Whitehead Island (near Argyle, in southwestern Nova Scotia).

It was October in the early 1950s and Ron was alone at the light—his father had taken a couple weeks' leave to go hunting. In fact, it was the night before his parents were to return to the island. A sudden thunderstorm moved in, pelting the island with rain and lighting up the sky with brilliant electric flashes.

In the lighthouse kitchen, Ron was busy trying to clean up the place after two weeks of bachelor life. "I was doing my dishes—I hadn't done them for three or four days, a week maybe, so I had to get things cleaned up before my father got back! It was just after supper and there come this bolt of lightning right between the house and the shed. It wasn't very far away!"

Shaken, Ron thought, "Any closer and this place'll be gone!" Seconds later there came a second smash. "I guess she's hit this time!" he remembered thinking. Ron quickly climbed the tower "to see what was goin' on. In the top room below the light itself, the plaster was all knocked offa the wall. I couldn't smell any smoke or anything, so I said, 'I guess it's alright,' and I went back downstairs and finished my dishes."

Drying his hands, Ron decided to climb the tower again. This time he knew he was in trouble. He could hear the fire in the walls, "snapping and cracking, like a fire in a stove." He ran outside, where he could now see flames licking the underside of the lighthouse lantern deck. There "wasn't a fire extinguisher in the whole place," so Ron grabbed a bucket from the kitchen and tried to fight the fire. No good. The tinder-dry wood in the seventy-year-old tower burned like a wildfire, spreading down the tower.

Ron knew by this time that the building was a lost cause, so he concentrated on hauling tables and chairs and other furniture out to the shed. Unknown to the young lad, people ashore in Argyle Sound had seen the fire—Bea, the woman who would later become his wife, remembers seeing a figure dashing between the lighthouse and shed, illuminated by jagged bolts of lightning.

Back out on the island, the weather was beginning to break. "By the time the fire was burning good, the stars was out," Ron remembered. "I just set back in the moonlight and watched 'er burn!"

Sitting in his kitchen in Argyle Sound more than half a century after the fire, Ron was pretty ho-hum as he described that night to me. "The old structure was a mess," he said. "It wasn't fit to live in anyway! It was no loss!" But his voice faltered as he talked about seeing his father. Two or three boats from Abbot's Harbour arrived around midnight that night, one of them bringing William Spinney. "I can still see him running over the side of the island…" Ron said, his voice trailing away. "I never thought of it at the time. I was fine, but they didn't know if I was dead or alive."

The Spinneys lived ashore while the Department of Transport built a new lighthouse. A short while after the fire, Ron received a letter from a man on Long Island, New York. It read:

Dear Mr. Spinney:

Your correspondent read of your recent adventure in one of our city's largest papers and thought you would like a copy for your own. New York is a huge and very impersonal place but its people are as human and warm as they are in Abbot's Harbour. Our city is a seaport and any tale of the Sea and men who make their living on or near it has a sincere audience. My best wishes to you and your heroic rescuers.

Respy,
W.B. Marks

Bea dug out the yellowed newspaper article from the *New York Herald-Tribune* to show me. Ron shook his head as I read the two-column story. It was written like a cheap melodrama, or a paperback cowboy novel, and most of it, Ron told me, was pretty well made up.

It had been a dirty day. At dusk a storm moved on in from the west. Ronald got the light going before he went for his own supper. As he finished the meal the sound of distant thunder coming closer was louder than the roar of the sea on the rocks. When the storm hit it hit hard and flaunted all its strength over White Head Light. A dozen lightning bolts snapped at the lighthouse before the biggest one struck it.

In the little frame house beside the beacon Ronald heard a crash and felt as if a giant bat had cracked his head. When he picked himself up, everything that could burn was afire and the beacon light was out. There was little he could save and he did not bother.

More head shaking from Ron, after all his efforts to remove furniture from the lighthouse! The story continued:

He stumbled to the radio transmitter to call help. He threw the switch but got no answering buzz. The set was dead. With fire burning all around on the little rock he ran out into the rain where lightning lit and relit the dark lighthouse and the flames flickered on the stone sides. Below him the sea on the rocks had the excited and triumphant roar of imminent victory.

Ron told me he couldn't remember it being an extraordinary evening weather-wise, aside from the thunderstorm and heavy showers. But what's a good sea story without some bad weather? According to the writer, Ron's rescuers had a bit of slop to deal with as they set out from Abbot's Harbour.

The waves came not in long high rollers but in angry disorderly moving mountains. Every man in each boat was soaking wet in a minute and holding to the gunwales for balance. Steering was tough. In those moments when sea or rain hid the blaze the boats started to come about against the sea. It took all the strength in the broad arms of the steersman to bring them back on course. No one spoke a word. No man could have heard a word if it had been said.

Finally, the men reached the island, where Ron, according to the writer, "crouched at the edge, waiting."

"Come, lad," one man said, as he helped the boy into the tossing boat. The craft turned about as the thunder roared and headed back to the mainland. The sea came angrily after them and the spume spattered the faces of the men like molten lead.

The story went on to say that "Sea stories out of Nova Scotia aren't scarce. Men there fight the sea as part of their daily work as men elsewhere get out of jams on the parkway or as others push through crowds."

Ron and I had a good laugh as we compared the newspaper story with what *really* happened the night the Whitehead Island light burned to the ground.

THEY WERE BLOWING HORNS AND SHOUTING FOR THEIR LIVES FOR THE KEEPER TO SAVE THEM.

From the earliest days of marine trade in eastern Canada, bad weather and shipwrecks went hand in hand. Even the lights built to guide steamers, schooners, and small fishing boats weren't proof against darkness and storm. Lightkeepers became first responders to shipwrecks, which often took place in their own front yards.

Stoic W. L. Munroe weathered many blows on Three Top Island in Guysborough County, hunkered down with his wife, Jane, and kids in a tiny wooden lighthouse barely out of reach of the Atlantic swells.

Munroe's biggest challenge came on a winter's night just before the dawn of the twentieth century. He wrote a dramatic account in the newspaper *Eastern Graphic*. It was Christmas Eve, and Munroe, his wife and a number of their ten children were just settling in the for the night.

> My wife and I went to bed about half past ten o'clock after seeing that Santa Claus was to visit the island and I suppose we had been retired about 20 minutes, when my wife aroused me by telling me that she heard a horn blowing. I told her she was dreaming, to go to sleep; but to please her I got up and went to the door to investigate.

> I found to my horror that she was right, for there on the reef that extends south east away from the mainland about two hundred yards lay a stranded vessel. They were blowing horns and shouting for their lives for the keeper to save them, as they thought from the way their ship was pounding she would break up, and certainly they would be doomed under such circumstances.

Munroe dressed and ran to the cliff, yelling that he would guide the men to shore by torch if they would take to their lifeboats. But it was impossible for the sailors to hear anything as the wind whistled in the wreck. But the keeper could hear the men, "their wailings…terrible to hear on such a night."

Munroe returned to the lighthouse, where he told his wife he was going to attempt "in God's name," to launch his boat to reach the stricken vessel. Munroe described his wife's reaction (in the male sensibilities of the day):

> As usual with women, my wife [was] crying and begging me not to dare such a thing on such an awful night and the chil-

dren, awakened by the tumult, [made] matters worse by joining their Ma in begging me not to go. I was pretty near abandoning the idea altogether until daylight. I went out of doors and down to the cliff. By the way their shoutings seemed to me, I imagined there were at least some of them in the water and perhaps drowning. I lit a fine torch, or flare up, as some call them and my wife following me, I went to the slip and let the boat down as far as I dared.

Immediately, Munroe was almost swept off the slipway in the heavy seas as his small boat turned bottom-up. Although that "pretty near discouraged me," the keeper decided to launch another small boat he had planned to use for lobster fishing in the spring.

Stoic lightkeeper William Munroe stands beside his wife, Jane.

I let the boat down part way this time, put my oars in her unhooked and sprung into the boat, taking chances going down the slip equal to "loop-the-loop'" and landed safe in the boiling water made by the gale. I grabbed my oars and as skilfully as I could managed my boat until I got out to the wreck, which I found to be the *George P. Trigg* from Charlottetown, PEI., bound to Boston, loaded with several thousand bushels of oats. She was trying to make the harbour to clear the storm when stranded. They had lowered the boat when first she struck the ledge and lost the boat in the sea. I found the men very much frightened. They all wanted to get in my small boat at once, but I told them to do as I told them and I would try to land them.

Munroe took three men at a time, not daring to let anyone touch his only set of oars, lest they be swept away by the seas. With Jane holding a torch to guide him to the island, Munroe began the several painstaking trips to pick up the crew, mate, and captain of the vessel. Finally, the exhausted keeper reached the island and landed safely.

> Thank God! We were all housed at 3 o'clock in the morning on Christmas Day. The wreck presented a gloomy-looking sight in the morning. The top of the hull which was above water, was a mass of ice, where no one could go near her for a couple of days.

Laurie Richardson Wickens (Anne Richardson's son) in the 1950s, sitting on one of the boilers from the SS *Express,* wrecked on Bon Portage Island in 1898. Shipwrecks at Nova Scotia lightstations were still common in the late nineteenth century.

THE WATER'S COMIN' IN OVER THE BOAT!

Grace (Shatford) Cahill saw her own lighthouse from a shipwrecked sailor's viewpoint one stormy night on St. Margaret's Bay, although her adventure had a happy ending. When I visited Grace at her home in Upper Tantallon, she sat me down in her kitchen and proceeded to regale me with all sorts of stories about life across the bay at the Hubbards lighthouse.

Grace's father, Oliver Shatford, his wife, Flora, and their eleven children lived at the lighthouse from 1912 to 1944. Grace wouldn't tell me how old she was, but she let me know that she could remember events from more than eighty years ago. It soon became obvious that her experience in a small boat on a squally night many years ago, was still fresh in her mind.

It had been a calm evening, with just a ripple on the waters off Hubbards. Grace's family was enjoying a visit from her brother Blaine, who was a sailor on a corvette moored in the bay. Tonight was a chance to catch up on news from the seagoing family member and give him a chance to stretch his legs on dry land. When Blaine asked if Grace

would row him out to the corvette—a half hour trip—at 10:00 P.M.,
Grace replied, "Sure! I don't mind a moonlight night."

It is useful to mention at this point that Grace's middle name
is Darling, and that her parents named her after England's famous
lighthouse heroine, immortalized in print (and on chocolate boxes!). In
1838, twenty-two-year-old Grace and her father, keeper of the Long-
stone lighthouse in Northumberland, rowed out in desperate sea conditions to rescue nine crew on the steamer Forfarshire, wrecked near the
lighthouse.

A century later, Oliver and Flora Shatford's little Grace Darling was
about to embark on her own little marine adventure. As the teenager
got ready to take her brother out to his ship, her brothers Neil and Alfie
decided to come along for company. When they reached the corvette,
brother Blaine climbed the rope ladder up the side of the ship, saying
"Thanks, be careful, take care," to the trio in the punt.

Grace told me, "We wasn't away from that boat ten minutes, when a
ragin' storm come. Every stroke you went ahead, the first thing you were
back three strokes. So I said, 'The water's comin' in over the boat."

The rough conditions didn't seem to bother young Grace. "Neil
used to say—he was nervous, and I don't think I was—'Boy, she's
some brave! But she won a couple swimmin' races!' But who could
swim in that? Each of them had two oars. I was sittin' in the end of
the boat, so I was facin' the shore. I said, 'Why don't you turn the boat
around and we'll land out in Bayswater or down somewheres along
the shore?'

But they were too close to shore to chance a change in course.
Grace had another idea to help them reach shore safely. "I started to
sing hymns. And the first thing I started to sing [was] 'Nearer My God
to Thee.' My brother said, "Grace, don't sing that. That's what they sang
in the Titanic!" Changing hymns, Grace launched into 'Farther Along,'
another old classic. Decades later she sat in her rocker by her gleaming
oil stove and sang for me in a cracked voice.

Cheer up my brother
Live in the twilight

We'll understand it
All by and by

Then she continued: "We finally made it home. Mama always left the lamp burning. We had no electric lights, you know. Well, boy oh boy, at twenty minutes to three, I woke her! We were *that* long gettin' in!

'Well', Mama said '*What happened?* Your eyes are wild!' I said, 'Mum, we were out to the boat till about ten o'clock, and we're just gettin' home!' Then Alfie said, 'Boy, you kept my spirits up, Grace.' I was just as frightened as Neil was!"

Rocking by the stove, looking back all those years, Grace laughed as she relived that stormy night. "Well, boys, it was awful! When I think about it now I could cry."

THIS THING'S GOT A MOVEMENT ALL OF HER OWN

Although most lighthouse people had experiences with shipwrecks or misadventures in small boats, they spent most of their time on dry land. But a select few kept the light burning and the horns blasting while pitching and rolling at sea. Such was life and work for the crew of the Sambro lightship.

From 1873 to 1966, a series of floating lighthouses welcomed all shipping to Halifax from a position south east of the Sambro Island lighthouse, beginning with lightship *Halifax* and ending with *Sambro Lightship Number 1*, which was finally replaced with a buoy.

Andy Hodder worked on the *Sambro Lightship* as a radio operator in the 1940s and '50s. While other crew members tended to the light and foghorn, Andy kept the ship's radio beacon operating and maintained a regular communications schedule with the mainland.

Month on, month off, for seven years, Andy endured the constant rolling of the lightship, anchored at the outer approaches to Halifax Harbour. And if the weather was sloppy, there wasn't anywhere to run. "You'd hear of a hurricane coming up the coast and you'd see all the

trawlers and all the ships heading for Halifax. But you stayed there," he told me. "Well, you were an aid to navigation so you had to be there! Just like an old buoy!"

The Sambro Lightship had "a movement all of her own."

As Andy told me, the ship had a "round bottom and she rolled from side to side. It was a peculiar motion, which took some getting used to." Newcomers wouldn't be aboard more than fifteen or twenty minutes and they'd get woozy. Even the old sea dogs, as Andy remembered: "One fella got all his discharge papers [record of ships served on] out and he said 'Here's twenty ships that I was on and I was never seasick. I get on a *pisspot* like this and I'm seasick!"

On another occasion an airline pilot spent some time on the lightship during some sloppy weather. "He was really, really mad to think that he would get in an aircraft, fly upside down, inside out, loops-theloop and never sick at all and then come out in a thing like a *lightship* and get sick! He was really, thoroughly done-in with himself!"

Andy laughed as he recalled the reaction of one of the lightship's skippers.

"We had a captain who was on old two- and three-masted schooners way back and he was on draggers. Captain Whynacht was his name. When he got aboard the lightship and was standin' there, he looks at me and he says, '*Tunderation!* This things's got a movement all of her own!'"

7

The Good, the Bad, and the Ugly

IN TALKING WITH MORE THAN SIXTY FORMER LIGHTKEEPERS and family members for this book—to say nothing of spending nine years as a keeper myself—I've come to the conclusion that there was very little middle ground in the lightkeeping experience. Sure, there were days of humdrum and routine, but lighthouse keepers and their families either really loved what they did, or they didn't care for it much at all.

I don't think I've ever heard some one say, "Oh, it was okay on the lights. I didn't mind it too much." Of course, the rose-coloured glasses syndrome comes into play in some cases. Time can soften the hard edges of a life that was isolating and unforgiving. But I get a sense of genuine affection for lighthouse life from almost everyone I interviewed, transcending reflective nostalgia.

Betty June, Anne, and Laurie Richardson enjoy the shoreline at Bon Portage Island.

Having grown up on McNutt's Island off Shelburne, Bernice Goodick had no illusions about the romance of lighthouse life. In the '40s and '50s, lightkeepers' salaries were low and the family had to scrape to make ends meet. But Bernice saw how good island life was when she finally had to move ashore.

"When I started high school, I realized that we were poor," she said to me. "I was fourteen in grade ten and I saw how the other kids dressed and what they had. I was so out of place."

So, it was dreadful for a while, for "the little country mouse in the big city." But then Bernice realized that island life had given her the spunk and the determination to succeed, even if she didn't have "two or three pairs of shoes or a dozen outfits!"

" I knew all the provinces, all the capitals, I knew all the counties in Nova Scotia and all the capitals. I knew my English, I knew my history. I could read and write French like a pro. Once I realized that I would use my assets and make the best of it, well, it was fun and I made friends and got along fine."

But Bernice also remembered that after coming ashore, her family was never as happy as they'd been on MacNutt's. Lighthouse life fostered, even demanded, close family ties. And for a child, there was almost complete freedom to roam coupled with unlimited opportunities for play.

For Kelly Fairservice, living on Sambro Island at the entrance to Halifax Harbour meant having "the most awesome playground anybody could ever have" right around her. "We lived over on the beach, building rafts and floatin' them out in the ocean," she said.

Island life meant extra responsibilities and worries for parents, but as Wick Lent told me, "you knew where your children were." Out at Brier Island's western light there was "plenty of open space and no danger." Well, no worry of getting run over by a bus, or suffering a neighbourhood bully, at least.

The work itself was appealing to men who liked to tinker and to those who took pride in keeping their stations painted and trimmed. Keepers like Waldo Haines, who didn't get into the job until later in life, said it was the best kind of work they could hope to get. Out on Cross Island, there was no frantic nine-to-five grind, no traffic gridlock at the end of the day. As long as the station was kept up and the light and the horn did their work, the keepers were free to do as they pleased. In short, it was the perfect place for Waldo, who told me, "we were never folks to gallivant around too much anyway!"

So it was a good life for a homebody who didn't mind that the home the body was parked on might be an island miles offshore. But what if that was not your cup of tea?

Surprisingly, of all the people I interviewed, very few had much bad to say about lighthouse life. But a tiny fraction—about three people— who did not enjoy the life expressed a surprisingly vehement dislike of the lighthouse experience.

For Melda and Marie Palmer, growing up at the Owl's Head light on the eastern shore meant social isolation and physical restriction. It was even hard to play around the house when you could hardly walk around it without tumbling down a granite cliff.

From a very early age both girls realized they wanted to get away from the lighthouse, despite being surrounded by a loving family. Melda remembers peering out her bedroom window at night, at the "big ships goin' way out to sea. I'd often wish I was old enough to get on one and go to never-never land!" she said ruefully.

Besides being cooped up in a house at the edge of a cliff, there were the added dangers of medical emergencies—especially in the days before radiotelephones and helicopters. It wasn't something lightkeepers dwelled upon, but if someone got hurt or needed a doctor, chances are they'd have to make do on their own.

On Flint Island, off Cape Breton's Port Morien, Brenton Hopkins became pretty adept at patching up his son Alf's scrapes and cuts. As Alf told me, "When you're out on an island like that with no one to depend on but yourself and whoever else happens to be there with you, you are a doctor, you are a lawyer, you're Indian chief, you're everything that there is. You get a cut, you don't go to the hospital. There is no hospital! You're five miles offshore in the middle of the Atlantic Ocean, so you fix it up!"

But when young Alf ran a high fever for days, he had to be taken ashore. Bundling the feverish boy into the boat, Brenton set off in a screeching gale. The trip to Port Morien took two and half hours, instead of the normal forty-five minutes, as mountainous seas smashed into the open twenty-eight-foot boat. Amazingly, Alf's fever broke on the way in. But there'd been no other choice—the keeper couldn't chance his son's life.

Good times or bad, a sense of humour was essential to existence on islands and remote headlands. Humour helped pass the time, and helped make light of tense situations. (It could also cause some tense times!)

Out on McNabs Island in Halifax Harbour, Glennie Cleveland delighted in a novel approach to decorating everyday life at home. She'd wait for a night when the lighthouse was bursting at the seams with family and visitors (usually soldiers from the nearby forts to see the bevy of comely young Cleveland girls) and then quietly steal upstairs to change into a pair of men's combination overalls. Then Glennie would slink back down the stairs and out the back door. Walking around to the front of the lighthouse, she'd knock loudly on the main door, asking for "so and so," when someone opened up. The deception didn't last long, and although a few soldiers were fooled, an explosion of laughter from Glennie or the family usually meant the jig was up.

Once on Flint Island, the lightkeepers took humour to another level, restraining a young fellow who occasionally worked as a fill-in keeper on the island, then applying black grease and soot to his nether regions. After freeing himself, the victim grabbed an axe and pursued his laughing attackers, who fled to opposite ends of the tiny island. All lived to tell the tale, and have, in fact, remained friends to this day!

I WOULDN'T TRADE MY CHILDHOOD FOR ANYBODY'S AROUND

Bernice Goodick spent the first sixteen years of her life on MacNutt's Island. In the 1940s the island was home to about twenty-five people—mostly fishermen and a couple of lightkeepers.

Before her family moved to the lighthouse, Bernice remembered regular visits for supper with head keeper Otis Orchard and his wife.

They'd been on the light since the thirties and Mrs. Orchard still didn't like it—as Bernice told me, she always said, "We're not living here, we're *staying*."

But they were hospitable folk, and it was a treat for Bernice and her brother to get an invite for a meal at the lighthouse. The big deal in those days was canned pears or peaches after supper, and hot biscuits.

Then, with full bellies, they'd walk home, "scared to death the whole way, singin' hymns because God's not gonna let anything hurt you, when you're singin' hymns! When you'd break over the hill and see that light shinin' out that window, you'd haul that door open and you'd rush in and slam it, and Mum would say, 'Well, it's good to have you home!'"

Bernice spoke emphatically about her life on MacNutt's Island. "I wouldn't trade my childhood for *anybody's* around! How many ten-year-olds have ever yoked up two oxen, or ridden through the island bareback on a horse, or walked through an island at twelve o'clock at night?"

The island community was close, and everyone pitched in to help their neighbours. If Douglas Renehan went to the mainland, he picked up everybody's mail. Bernice remembers that islanders "used to call Dad the mayor. When he got all cleaned up on a Sunday morning, shave and everything, he'd look in the mirror and say, 'There, best lookin' man on the island!'

"I'd say, 'Well Dad, there's only Mr. Orchard and Mr. Hemeon besides you and they're ugly as sin, so you pretty well gotta be the best lookin' man on the island!'"

In the 1950s the Renehans moved to the lighthouse, where Douglas had been appointed assistant keeper. On a small salary it was still lean times, but Bernice's parents were resourceful—relatives from Cape Sable Island would send down a barrel of old clothes and her mother would cut them into strips to make quilts. Douglas had a fair hand with a needle, making clothes and little rag dolls for the kids.

In the evenings, when Douglas was on watch, Bernice and her mother made the little trek to the fog alarm building. Amidst the clamour of fog alarm engines, they'd play cards, yelling at each other to be heard over the blasts of the horn and the growling engines.

Bernice told me about holing up in the engine room during

thunder storms—when her father had to keep an extra close eye on the machinery—and she delighted in the lightning that would "come in and play around the engines. Little blue chains would go from engine to engine and snap and crackle."

She added, "Today I'd be scared of course, but back then I thought it was great!"

And so, it appears, was life on Cape Roseway. When I asked Bernice what the best thing about living on the island was, she mentioned a warm home, a close family…and chocolate.

"Every night in the winter Mum would get out the slab bar—they were about a foot long, chocolate, with nuts and raisins in little sections. We had two squares each evening. You looked forward to that all day because that was your treat for the night."

It's often the little things that stand out when you cast your mind back to the cozy days of childhood. But children grow and as they get bigger, islands grow smaller. Then comes the day when they have to leave.

For Bernice, the worst part of island life was thinking, "There's gotta be something better'n this in the outside world." The Renehans finally moved to that "outside world" in 1956. Bernice's mother was ill, and it was time to move ashore. It was a big change for the whole family. Bernice and her mother had both been born and raised on the island, and it took some doing to fit into mainland life.

As Bernice remembered, "The very worst part was findin' out that everybody else wasn't like you. That you were different. You had a different upbringing. You were never as casual about anything as what other people were. You never took anything for granted. Mum always said, 'Don't worry about what you don't have. Be thankful for what you *do* have.'

"So I was always sort of like a Pollyanna. I've always been an optimist and you know, sometimes you do stick out. I have been noted to be outspoken. Sometimes my foot is in my mouth more than it's in my shoe. But that's what we were taught. Dad always said, 'If you're right, never give in, never give up on an argument. If you're wrong, be man enough to apologize.' But it took a long time for me to learn that!" she added, laughing. "I was always right, no matter what! Still am!"

AN ADVENTURE EVERY DAY

For the Barkhouse family, island life was one big adventure. David and Jean began their lightkeeping journey in 1951, on Lunenburg's Cross Island. A few years later they moved to Maugher's Beach in Halifax Harbour. They bounced back to Cross Island, and later to Pearl Island, off Mahone Bay.

Dave went out to replace Albert Pearl, who had mysteriously disappeared on a cold January day in 1962. No one ever found a trace of the keeper, aside from a partly eaten meal left on the table.

Jean wasn't too crazy about Pearl Island. It was and is a rugged spot—a flat-topped, wind-swept chunk of real estate where the original lighthouse was held to the ground with thick cables. It was also a tough place to get on and off, and Jean was always worried about the safety of her three young children. But as daughter Patti remembered, nobody wore a lifejacket. Most people didn't in those days, before safe-boating courses and due diligence. "Those were stuffed down in the bow of the boat, 'cause they got in the way!" she recalled.

Jean and the kids didn't move out to the island until the summer of 1962. When school started in the fall, she took the children back to the family home in Mahone Bay, returning to the island to visit Dave on weekends and holidays. Landing on the island was always a tricky operation in a place where the sea was never calm.

Smashing through the swells, they'd finally reach the northern end of the island where there was a small slipway and a boathouse. So far so good, but actually setting foot on the island first meant putting everyone aboard a small dory, pulling through the heaving seas and waiting for the right wave to deposit them on the slip.

For the unwary there'd be a sudden "Hold on!" from Dave. No other explanation was forthcoming, as Dave "wasn't one to explain things." The surge would drive the little boat onto the poles and then the whole thing would tip to one side, while its wet and trembling passengers scrambled for safety.

The Barkhouse kids loved having the run of the island, but it was a constant worry for Jean, who wasn't keen on living so close to an unpredictable sea. During a hurricane, Patti and her brother Lawrence stayed glued to the lighthouse windows, watching waves that "looked like mountains" charging towards them. There'd a be a chorus of "Ohhh, here comes another one," and two little faces with wide eyes laughing with delight as the water swirled around the foundation of their home.

Jean was pregnant at the time, and not particularly in the mood for seas hitting the house. She decided to make bread to take her mind off the sea and her bouncing kids. It didn't work. Jean was frightened by the waves, "three and four behind one another that would come up and wash around the house like if the house itself was an island! No thank you—that's not for me!"

Retreating upstairs to lie down, Jean tried to escape her childrens' continued excitement. Forty years later, she laughed and said, "I was not *excited*. I was *terrified!*"

Things were soon to get better. After less than a year, Dave got a transfer to Georges Island in Halifax Harbour. Now they were going to be an "urban" lighthouse family, living on a tiny island just off Pier 21 in the heart of the harbour.

No more tortuous boat trips, no more waves hitting the house. Georges was a little jewel in the harbour, with its white lighthouse, keepers bungalow and abandoned fortifications, set amidst lush grass and rose bushes.

At the end of the school year Jean and the kids joined David and his assistant on the island. From then until September it was non-stop beachcombing, boat-watching, and playing in the labyrinth of tunnels running through the island. Patti remembers pretending to play in a band with her brothers, where "the lights from Halifax and Dartmouth was the audience sitting out there with their lighters."

Today Patti and Bobby agree that island life gave them freedom and adventure, whether it was creeping along the dark dripping tunnels with a flashlight, or being almost dumped into the harbour while being pushed along the wharf in a wheelbarrow. As Patti remembered, "you just got to be a kid."

Farther down the eastern shore on Beaver Island, it was a pretty good life for Blair and Joyce Cameron's seven kids. In the 1960s the lightstation was a little village in its own right, with three keepers and their families living around the tower.

Blair kept busy tending the light and keeping the buildings painted. He also kept an eye on his own kids, and those of one of the assistants. On one occasion the assistant's boys decided to smash dozens of two-hundred-watt light bulbs. Blair's solution was to hang the culprits "up on the clothesline for half the night."

Blair wasn't in good health when I spoke to him in the spring of 2004, his stories trailing off into fits of coughing, but he laughed as he thought back forty years and told me the boys "didn't think much," of being strung up. "When I let them down they come after me with a big long pole. If they'd a' hit me I'd a' been gone long before I was!"

"Bad buggers," he added. "The whole tribe of them!"

His own kids weren't angels either. Aside from liberating various supplies to use in the construction of forts, they got into the usual sky-larking that many do, whether on an island or ashore.

Valerie liked to steal Ruth Fleet's bread. The assistant keeper's wife often set her freshly baked efforts out on the kitchen counter—Valerie had a habit of coming into the house and grabbing a couple of buns before it got that far. Ruth "used to like to wait for her bread to cool off," Valerie told me, "but I wanted it hot!" When finally caught, Valerie received a whack with "some kind of a paddle." After that, she had to settle for cooler bread.

For the most part, Beaver Island families got along well, visiting in the evenings, playing cards and occasionally attending plays in the light-house. All the families showed up, cramming into the bottom floor of the little wooden lighthouse to watch the kids' theatrical productions—usually based on the trouble the kids got into and, as Valerie remembers, "how we would get out of it."

Boredom was an unknown condition for the Cameron kids, with other kids to play with, picnics on the beach, swims in the icy cold Atlantic, and camps constructed in secret spruce groves. As Valerie said, "it was an adventure every day."

Laurie, Betty June, and Anne Richardson with their indispensible ox playmate.

For Anne, Laurie, and Betty June Richardson the adventure included large and four-legged playmates. Some were to be trusted, others not. Amaryllis the cow, with her misleadingly pretty name, was a "hateful creature," as Anne remembered. "We were all warned against her and never went around her. Dad didn't even put the other cows with her!"

Amaryllis added a little excitement to an already hectic time when she decided to strangle herself during Laurie's birth. The field where the cow spent much of her time grazing was very close to the Richardsons' lighthouse home. "It was a rather interesting session, from what I gather," Anne told me. "It was a very hard birth and in the middle of it, Amaryllis wrapped the rope around her own throat and lay down and started rolling around.

"The midwife screamed, the doctor dropped everything and went rushing out. He didn't know what to do for the cow. The midwife came tearing out with a carving knife and cut the rope."

Fortunately Laurie arrived without further mishap.

Broad the ox, on the other hand, was much too gentle and sensible to be interfering with childbirth and other important happenings. He seemed to have a thoughtful outlook, as Anne and Laurie climbed up one side of him and slid down the other. Pensively chewing his cud, he endured and perhaps even enjoyed the attention. After climbing over his horns and sliding down his nose, the kids would "whack him right in the eyes because the flies liked to get in his eyes and we didn't want them to do that," according to Anne.

"Broad was seldom in the lighthouse field (we were not allowed out of it) except for those noons on which he was required for an afternoon shift," Anne later wrote. "Mother, most unreasonably, insisted on a full hour for dinnertime—Dad would have leaped to his feet and gone to work at the last swallow. It would have done no good to tell him he *must* take a break; Mother argued that it wasn't fair to the hired man. Dad fidgeted, grumbled, but finally adjusted to a few minutes' relaxation after his meal.

"That was when we revelled with Broad, for apparently no adult ever learned of it!"

.22S AND TEA TOWELS

It didn't hurt to have a sense of humour living on a lighthouse. The old saying, "Might as well laugh as cry," made a lot of sense when life was hard. And lighthouse life was tough, especially in the days before insulated houses, electricity and helicopters. It was a constant struggle to keep houses warm when the searching winds of winter sent icy fingers through rattling windows and doors.

"Man, the crows could fly right straight through this place and it wouldn't bother them a bit," Jim Guptill's father liked to say as the family shivered in the old Country Island lighthouse. But Keith Guptill and most other keepers were stoics, facing the challenges with acceptance and dry humour.

Even Melda (Palmer) DeBaie, who hated living at Owl's Head, laughed when she talked about her life there. It was a lonely time for

The Guptill children in front of the old Country Island lighthouse, which was drafty enough that "the crows could fly straight through…and it wouldn't bother them a bit!"

a young girl, stuck out on that rock, always mindful of the sea below the cliffs. Melda told me that living at Owl's Head made her "scared of a lot of things after I grew up. I was scared of heights, scared of gettin' drownded," she told me. "I was born and brought up in a boat, but I'm scared to death of one! I remember when I was five or six, there used to be the RCMP Marine Division. They'd come in a white cutter and anchor offa the light. They'd dig up all the turf and they'd dig up the rock—they were lookin' for the bootleg rum at that time. Mum used to keep me and me brother pretty well straight that week. She'd say, 'If you fellers is not good, I'm goin' give you away to the Mounties!'"

She grinned at me. "All I have to do today is look at a Mountie and I freeze!"

Melda still found time for a bit of fun with her sister Marie and helping her brother John snare rabbits and playing on the flat area on the landward side of the lighthouse. Sometimes the play even involved firearms.

"Me brother took Dad's .22 one time. I might have been ten and he might have been twelve. I don't know what he was going to shoot, but he wouldn't let me have it. Whew! We got in some fight. Wonder he hadn't 'a shot me, the way we were wrasslin' over this gun!"

Out on McNutt's Island, Bernice (Renehan) Goodick's mother was often curious as to why her tea towels always seemed to develop holes as they hung on the clothesline. The Christmas delivery of two Daisy BB guns may have had something to do with it. Bernice also had an interest in larger calibre firearms and, along with her brother, she whiled away the odd day at target practice.

"We used to line up the empty cartridges on the stone wall," she told me, "and we would stand by the porch, and we would shoot them over. We were both good shots. But we didn't use them as toys. We didn't point them at each other or anything, we just used them for practice. We never shot birds or anything like that, with our BB rifle or .22s. I tried shootin' Dad's rifle one time, but I think that's what the matter with my shoulder now, because it knocked me ass-over-kettle!"

Out at Chebucto Head, little Sara Flemming used a little educational salesmanship to pass the time and earn a little pocket money. In the late fifties and early sixties people began to drive out to the light to enjoy the view and perhaps a little snuggle time in a cozy parked car. It was a great business opportunity for the spunky kid.

"I'd knock on the car window and say, 'Hi, I'm Sara, I'm from the light, I've lived there all my life. The reflector is floated on a half a ton of mercury…" and they would say, 'Yeah, that's really nice. Here's a quarter. Go home!'"

There wasn't much chance for romance when Sara was around.

Sara also had a dream of seeing her name in lights. To that end, she borrowed a bit of electrician's tape and taped her initials on the large bulb in the middle of the catoptric reflector at the top of her home. For a while at night a huge "S. F." projected out over the harbour approaches, like an oversized version of shadow puppets. The experiment came to an abrupt end when her father, Stanley, noticed his daughter's "half-mile high," initials in the night sky and instructed Sara "to get it off there *immediately!* It was like the Batman signal over

Gotham City!" she cackled. "It was something I probably shouldn't have done, but it *needed* to be done at the time!"

SLINGSHOTS AND SEALS

Extreme conditions at some of the more isolated lights may have encouraged slightly more aggressive ways of passing the time. Faced with the daily challenges of temperamental machinery, rugged shores and constant maintenance, some keepers seemed to need a release from the labour and routine.

Flint Island fit into the "extreme" mode, both in its exposed location off the east coast of Cape Breton and in the character of some of its inhabitants.

In the 1950s and early '60s, Flint's head keeper was Brenton Hopkins. When it came to work, Hopkins was a full-tilt, no-nonsense kind of man who attacked all tasks with vigour and purpose. He also attached the same energy to the occasional prank.

Take the seal-in-diapers incident, for instance. Brentons's son Alf told me that a certain young man known as Junior was a regular visitor to the island. Apparently he was a sound sleeper, and difficult to rouse in the morning. Undaunted by this, Brenton devised a creative way of getting the lad out of bed.

On the morning in question, a few Harp seals were hanging around below Flint's red mud cliffs. Brenton observed this, and, according to his son, "went down and he molly-grubbed this thing, got it up over the bank and had it up on the doorstep.

"They got it into their heads, the old man and my Uncle Hughie, that they were gonna put this seal in bed with Junior. Dad got a piece of canvas, made up a diaper, put this diaper on the seal, and they carried it upstairs and they put in bed with Junior."

Brenton and Uncle Hughie carried their little diapered bundle of joy quietly up the stairs and carefully slid him into bed with the sleeping young man. Junior sniffed and snuffled and shifted in bed. The seal wriggled closer for a whiff of human. Junior sniffed again.

Hmm. Fishy smell. Strange dream.

But it was no dream. Nose-to-nose contact did the trick. Junior awoke suddenly, face to whiskered snout. Eyes wide, "he came *straight* up out of the bed," as Alf recalled. "The bedclothes rose, he went out from under the bedclothes, and the bedclothes settled back down on the bed again. Then he's tearin' downstairs. He's in his underwear. Aunt Betty and the whole bunch of the women were downstairs titterin' and goin' on. So now he's caught between the rock and a hard place, 'cause he can't run downstairs, 'cause he's the best part of naked and he has to go back upstairs, but he don't know what the *hell* that was in the bed!"

Seals in diapers notwithstanding, even Brenton had his limits when it came to hijinks. One day, another family friend who spent time on the island in the summer found a substantial tree-crotch washed ashore. When it comes to slingshots, size matters, and in no time Georgie had the Y-shaped trunk firmly anchored in the ground and made fast to a fence at the edge of the cliff.

Finding the elastic for a huge slingshot on a tiny island in the Atlantic was no problem, as Alf told me. "They used to make their own belts for the engines. Part of the material that they had was this red, red rubber. This stuff was pretty stretchy. [Friends and the assistant would] go down and get beach rocks, *big* beach rocks. They'd pull back on this red rubber just as hard as they could and they'd let these beach rocks go, cripes, hundred of yards out into the water!"

Beach rocks were one thing. Human projectiles were another.

"Dad looked out one day and they had Georgie in the sling! He had to jump out and holler and screech and get them to stop doin' what they were doin'. I don't know if they would have let him go or not, but in all likelihood, he would have got wet that day! If it hadn't a' killed him!"

BETTER KNIGHTS AND BETTER LADIES

Other lighthouse people were known for their gentler senses of humour. Along with being affectionate to his loving children, Morrill Richardson was a very courteous man. After *We Keep A Light* came out in 1945, people started to visit Bon Portage Island to meet his now-famous wife Evelyn. But as Anne remembered, "all the little old ladies fell in love with him. There was just no resisting him!"

Morrill Richardson also had what Anne described as a "quirky sense of humour, which tickled some people, although some people just looked at him with a very blank stare!"

Evelyn also had a good sense of humour and "sort of put up with Dad's," according to Anne. She told me her father would always indicate that *he* had taught his wife how to cook. (This claim was in spite of all the rushing about in the kitchen and clouds of flour during Morrill's memorable cookie-baking incident when Evelyn was ill in bed. Betty June tactfully described the incident: "Daddy is a very energetic cook. Sometimes I think he uses too much energy and not enough discretion.")

Once, a visiting Aunt Lillian said she'd "discovered how to keep baking powder going till you got to the end of the can. There was one ingredient heavier than the others, so if you turned the can over and shook it the heavy stuff would start sinking back again. Mother said, 'Oh, how wonderful, because my biscuits are never what they ought to be when I get down to the bottom of the can!'"

To which Morrill responded: "Well now Evelyn, you *haven't* been to blame all these years. I never told you *that!*"

Morrill was also known for his puns. One glorious summer evening he stood on the back porch of the lighthouse with Mildred Ritcey, a distant relation to Evelyn and one of her closest friends. As the stars twinkled in a velvet sky and the moon shimmered across the sound, Muriel sighed and declared, "Ohhh Morrill, *what* a night!"

Not one to miss a beat, Morrill replied, "I've seen better *knights*, and better ladies!"

As Anne recalled, "Aunt Mildred went in and burst into tears!" Between "awful sobs" she told Evelyn what was wrong. "Mother was annoyed at Dad," Anne said, "but she didn't know whether to give Dad a blast, or laugh!"

Fortunately she took to laughing, saying "Oh Mildred, it wasn't what you think. It was just one of his *puns!*" But as Anne told me, poor

Aunt Mildred "never seemed to get the hang of the fact that Dad was sort of pulling her leg!"

Glennie Cleveland was a great leg puller in her own right. Mother to seven children and the gregarious wife of quiet and calm Colin, Glennie delighted in livening up life on McNabs Island. Not that it was a quiet place. During World War Two, dozens of soldiers and officers staffed the island's forts and maintained a submarine net from Maugher's Beach across to the fort at York Redoubt.

Soldiers often visited the Clevelands' lighthouse, where a full table and an evening of music were a welcome diversion from official duties. It was also the perfect venue for Glennie, as her daughter Joan remembered when I spoke with her.

"Marjorie was the oldest girl and mother used to try to get Marjorie married off. This was the family joke." But Glennie had funny ways of assessing the suitor's suitability. Joan continued: "Mother was always instigating. Anyway, Mack, the sailor, was having supper with us. He's sitting around this table with all these people and they're all strangers to him. He's gonna have to be on his best behaviour. But my mother wasn't on her best behaviour! She poured a glass of vinegar into a wine glass and passed it to him. We're all having a toast and 'course we can all see this! Meanwhile, he's making up to this young lady and he has to do *everything* right!

"Down went the glass of 'wine.' Well, poor man, he nearly died! It nearly choked him! So that was always a family joke, how mother tried to do him in!"

There was another incident involving Mack, some cheese and some Ex-Lax, but it didn't put the young sailor off track. He and Marjorie were soon married and when I spoke with Joan in the fall of 2002, Mack had just turned eighty and was living with his sweetheart in California.

Sundays were a bit quieter in the Cleveland household. After Colin had put out the light for the morning, the family would have breakfast and then settle down to listen to a church service on the radio. Colin would have preferred a quiet day of reflection, but Glennie didn't sit still for long, even on a Sunday.

Youngest daughter Faye told me that Glennie would sneak down to Fort Hugonin on the island's north end, to visit with the fort's caretakers, the Willses. They enjoyed a good game of Rumoli, as did Glennie Cleveland. "Dad didn't really believe in gambling," Faye continued. "He didn't mind so much them playing cards during the week, but Sundays he really didn't think they should be playing cards. He knew Mum did, but he just used to pretend he didn't."

As Glennie and the Willses covertly played Rumoli, Colin Cleveland would decide to pay a visit. "He'd make all kinds of noise so that they would know he was coming. Mr. Wills would look out and see Dad. 'Oh, my God, Mr Cleveland!' All the money would go flying and the Rumoli board would be put away and they'd be there sedately having a nice visit!"

I LOST MY CHILDHOOD

Lighthouse life wasn't all roses. For families stuck out on barren headlands and islands, distance from civilization and lack of amenities sometime took their toll. Although many took the life in stride, a few cultivated a strong dislike of the lighthouse experience.

In some ways it was a breath of fresh air to talk with Melda and Marie Palmer. From the very beginning, both ladies made it perfectly clear that they were not going to wax romantic about their early days at the Owl's Head light.

"It was horrible!" That's how Marie described the place as I talked with her in a comfortable seniors apartment overlooking Eastern Passage and the expanse of Halifax Harbour. Sitting in a recliner and holding a binder of family history, she admitted that for her father John, who had eked out a living working in the woods and as a cook at sea, it was a welcome chance for a steady paycheque and a warm house for his wife and eight kids.

But for young Marie and her sister, Owl's Head lighthouse was an isolated prison from which they could not wait to escape. Not that it was so bad at first. Marie was four years old in 1925, when the family moved to the lighthouse, and she was excited. "I thought I was going *somewhere*," she remembered with a laugh. But somewhere turned into nowhere after a few years.

The light sat on the edge of a cliff, so the kids couldn't even run around their home. It meant that Etta Palmer had to keep a close eye on her kids while trying to do the myriad of chores needed to keep a household of eleven (a cousin lived with the family as well) warm and properly fed.

A few days after talking with Marie I found myself sitting with her sister Melda in her quiet Dartmouth apartment. Not one to beat around the bush, Melda gave me *her* first impressions of Owl's Head: "I suppose I might have been three or four before I woke up and seen where I was! I thought that's all there was to the world, was that rock and the ocean!"

Isolated from her school chums (it was a six mile round-trip walk to the main road to the village of Owl's Head) and confined to the house in the winter, Melda soon decided that this was not the life for her. "I remember one time Mum was rockin' me, out there in that little porch. I must have only been five, because I looked up in her face and I said, 'Mum, how many more years before I'll be me own boss?'"

Etta answered, "Sixteen more years," before calling her husband in to hear what their precocious daughter had just said. "You'll never believe what that young one asked me!"

John replied "God knows what *she'd* say!"

"Well," said Etta, "she asked me how long would it be before she'd be her own boss!" "Sixteen years!" was John's reply as well. (In those days, twenty-one was the magic age of independence.)

Seventy-three years later, Melda lit a cigarette and laughed ruefully. She'd left the lighthouse at fourteen—"The war had just broke out and somebody told me there were money and jobs out there. Happiest day of me life!"—and went to work in a woodworking factory in Ship

Marie (Palmer) Stevens on life at Owl's Head lighthouse: "I can say it wasn't all that bad. But not that good, either!"

Harbour. Working there until "the great old age of nineteen," she got married. By the time Melda was old enough to be her own boss she had one baby and another on the way.

"So whose boss was I then?" she asked me, though it was more of a statement. "I lost me childhood. It's laughable, but it was sad."

You didn't have to be three miles from the nearest road to have a dislike of lighthouse life. The seeds of discontent could grow just as well on an island in the middle of Halifax Harbour. Georges Island was home to Dale (Matthews) Veinot for almost two decades. Even though the family lived just a five minute boat ride from bustling Halifax, Dale found life on the tiny, grassy islet oppressive. Sure, Fort Charlotte's tunnels were just asking to be explored and yes, Dale had a front row seat to watch ocean liners and cargo ships.

But life was primitive—no electricity and coal heat, even though the Matthewses' house was just a stone's throw from the huge power station near Pier 21. "We had to clean the chimneys on the lamps all the time," Dale said. "It was very hard to read by those lamps. Then you'd have to iron with those old irons heated on a stove and I burned somebody's shirt when I did!"

There were regular trips to the city for school and church, but other than that, Dale said, "we never went anywhere. We never travelled, we just stayed there. I had a different life. My parents were very religious so we weren't allowed to do anything. I wasn't allowed to dance and go to shows, so I just spent most of my time in Fort Charlotte."

When I spoke to her more than forty years after she left Georges, Dale's dislike of island life had morphed into something much different. She was intensely proud of her connection to the island, always anxious to tell people just what it was like to live there, warts and all. "I run down to Pier 20 now and then" she said, "and look out to the island and wish that I could go back and live there, my husband and I, as caretakers, when they restore the fort."

WIPIN' THE TEARS DOWN FROM HER FACE

There were certain facets of lighthouse life that made the experience diverse and challenging, whether you liked the life or not. Aside from the regular struggles against wind and waves, there was the issue of medical emergencies. If you were ill or hurt, how did you get help, living at the end of a three-mile goat track, or even worse, a dozen miles from the mainland?

Evelyn Richardson bemoaned the lack of a telephone during the family's early years on Bon Portage. The family had to rely on a red flag hung from the clothesline or a blaze of oil-soaked rags to signals friends in Shag Harbour if they needed help.

Even if you were a scant mile from shore, getting medical help could be a dicey business. In 1935, Russ Latimer's thirteen-year-old sister died in part because of what Russ briefly described as "a lack of expediency and proper medical diagnosis." After Marjorie Latimer took sick, her father rowed his daughter to the station motorboat, then made the mile-and-a-half trip to the point where she was hoisted aboard the Canso–Mulgrave supply steamer. Some hours later, Marjorie was put aboard the train to Antigonish, but it was too late. She died on the way to the hospital.

It was a huge blow to Dorothy Latimer, losing her only daughter. And fate had another trial in store. That same year, Russ's younger brother, Lloyd, fell into the cold waters of Crid Pass when he was blown off the slipway by a gust of wind. The three-year-old floated face down, buoyed by a pocket of air in the seat of his overalls.

Russ later wrote to me about the incident: "When we retrieved him from the water we noticed that his body was limp and lifeless. My mother rolled Lloyd's body, stomach downward, over a nearby net keg that was on the beach and I dashed across in a rowboat and ran to the village to find the local doctor—Arichat's *only* doctor."

After an interminable two-hour wait, as Dorothy Latimer tried to revive her son, Russ and the doctor reached the island "to find Lloyd beginning to show life signs. The doctor indicated to my mother that through her endeavours she had saved the baby's life."

There was no such happy ending at the Owl's Head lighthouse in late 1927. Melda Palmer was only a year and a half old at the time, but she swears she can remember the day her baby brother died. His name was Scott Lewis Palmer, and he lived for only ten days.

"I wasn't allowed in Mum's bedroom," she told me. "They had it locked. The baby had some kind of a blockage in its esophagus. If it hadda been in this day and age they'd 'a sent a helicopter out and he 'a been transferred right into the children's hospital, so he probably would have lived. I think he just starved to death, 'cause he couldn't suck or he couldn't swallow."

Melda's siblings have told her there's no way she can remember that day. But she's adamant that she does. With closed eyes, she recalled for me the heartbreaking scene. "I can see the livin' room, I can see me father, he was cryin' and Marcelle me older sister—she was about twelve or thirteen—she had me on her lap, tryin' to jam this bottle in me mouth. I wasn't about to go to sleep and I remember me takin' me little hands and wipin' the tears down from her cheeks."

Little Scott's death left a grieving mother, father, and siblings, but the Palmer family stuck it out at Owl's Head. Although Melda and her sister Marie left as soon as they were in their mid-teens, Etta Palmer and her husband stayed at Owl's Head until John retired in the 1950s. But the loss of their baby was always with them.

Tragedy also marked the otherwise happy life of the Munroe family on White Head Island in 1924. The low, scrubby, and fogbound island marks the entrance to White Head Harbour in Guysborough County. On an early June day, one of the Munroe boys left the island for an appointment with the dentist, leaving lightkeeper Almon with his oldest son Lee. During that evening one of the area's frequent easterlies began to batter the island with dense fog and rain.

Two hours before the midnight watch change, Almon summoned his son. He was feeling terrible, vomiting, and he had to get to bed. He left his son with instructions to start the foghorn, and then, doubled over in pain, made his way through the storm to his warm house.

Through the night Lee kept the grease cups full on the foghorn engines and kept an exhausting watch over the light, winding the clock-work mechanism, checking kerosene levels and pumping the air for the vapour burner.

Rugged White Head Island in 1978, more than half a century after keeper Almon Munroe died on the station.

The storm raged on through Friday, Saturday, and Sunday. There was no way to contact anyone ashore. The lighthouse distress signal—a flag raised half-mast from a pole on the highest point on the island— was of no use. Who would see it in the tempest?

The constant foghorn duty and worry over his father soon began to wear on Lee. As his sister Mary-Ellen later wrote in her memoirs, "My brother, tired right down to the bone, exhausted from no sleep, having eaten but little, sat on the step and cried. 'If the weather doesn't soon clear they will find both of us dead!'"

Finally, on Monday, the weather cleared enough to shut down the foghorn. Almon, still in his sick bed, waited patiently for his son to return from the mainland. That afternoon he arrived after bucking his way through foaming seas to find his father deathly ill and Lee at the point of collapse.

He returned to the mainland at once to find the doctor. Mary-Ellen wrote, "Can you picture this scene? The doctor was fifteen miles from the village, the island was at least three miles by water, and then the walk across the island?"

After all that, it was too late. Almon Munroe died just as the doctor arrived. Mary-Ellen was waiting at the family's mainland home. Running to the shore at the sound of her brother's boat, she "heard him crying so I knew my father had died. I shall never forget the scene of the arrival of the casket," she wrote. "There it was, a grey boat towing a dory with my father's casket and the flag at half mast." Lee and his brothers stayed on at the light for another two years, until the Department of Marine and Fisheries could find a new keeper. Mary-Ellen wrote that after her father's death, "the island seemed a lonelier spot," and that her family was glad to leave. "The island, with its roaring breakers, wild ocean, and its everlasting fog…was only to be enjoyed in [our] youth."

A RUGGED AND HEALTHY LIFESTYLE

Through the tragedies and the laughter, everyone who lived on the lights came away with a lesson or an appreciation for the experience— whether it was for a glorious summer evening, or a last look at a light you couldn't wait to get away from.

When I look back, Russ Latimer comes closest to tying it all together, weathering the inconveniences and tragedies of island life with acceptance and fortitude. Dropped into island life in 1930, at the age of ten, Russ rose to the challenge.

"It was a matter of integrating into the fact that there was no playing ever done," he said to me. "There was nothing to play with or at. So, it was all work—mere existence at the lighthouse entailed a combined effort on the part of the entire family."

Obviously there was no time for sports, but Russ got enough exercise on land and on the water. "I suppose I excelled at yachting (as it is known today) because I did a lot of sailing, as an alternative to rowing," he said.

Being on the water also gave Russ the chance to earn some pocket money. At thirteen, he desperately wanted a bicycle. In the absence of a weekly allowance, Russ tumbled out of bed at 4:30 in the morning, piled into a row boat, and hauled fifty lobster traps by hand—every day before rowing to school.

By season's end in 1933, young Russ had raised the magnificent sum of twenty-one dollars to buy his coveted *Canadian Winner* from the T. Eaton catalogue. "This was indeed a highlight of my life," Russ later wrote to me. "After having risen early each day, developing a ravenous appetite and great muscles, I consider it was a rugged and healthy lifestyle."

It wasn't *all* work. In the evenings, the family clustered around the kitchen table to listen to the radio, sharing the single earpiece. Russ recalled the first radio signal he ever heard. "Hello, this is VAS, Voice of the Atlantic Seaboard, at Glace Bay, Nova Scotia," beamed magically into the tube radio in the lighthouse.

Without an external speaker in the radio, the Latimers had to squeeze around the kitchen table and share an earpiece to catch a snippet of whatever was on—maybe *Amos and Andy*, or the *Major Bowes Amateur Hour* (which debuted on NBC in 1935—"desperate" performers converged on New York for their shot at stardom. Many of the yodelling, tap-dancing, and whistling hopefuls were "gonged" off the show, a trick later made popular in TV's *Gong Show*), or Lowell Thomas's authoritative baritone saying, "Good evening everybody" as he prepared to read the day's news on NBC.

Sid Smith and a friend tune into a radio show at Cape Sable in the 1950s. Radio was a big part of lighthouse life, especially before the 1950s, when television started to take over.

Commercials were few but memorable. "Pepsodent toothpaste, Jello with its five flavours: strawberry, raspberry, orange, lemon, and lime. I can hear it now," Russ later wrote. "Then there were Lucky Strike cigarettes, so round, so firm, so fully packed, and so *delicious*! No wonder I learned to become a veteran smoker!"

Even Melda and Marie Palmer, who couldn't wait to leave their lighthouse home, dredged up a few good memories of the old days. Melda laughed when I asked her what she thought about when she cast her mind back to her days at Owl's Head. "Well, I think I'm some goddamn glad I'm not there no more!" But, she added, "I wouldn't mind goin' back out, but not in a boat and then up those cliffs. And the road is all grown over."

Melda admitted to having had a "little twinge of sorrow" when years later her mother phoned to say the Coast Guard had burned the lighthouse to the ground. "But it was nothin' I could cry over," she said. "It was too late then."

Marie added, "For myself, I always felt cheated not being able to get an education. But my children and grandchildren have all done well and that makes me happy. So I feel more mellow towards the lighthouse at eighty-two years old.

"I can say it wasn't all that bad. But not that *good*, either!"

8

~

Strange and Wonderful

PICTURE AN ISOLATED ISLAND, A STORMY NIGHT, WITH the petrels crying as they fly in the beam of the light. A solitary keeper stares into the inky blackness with only hot rum and an overactive imagination for company.

The scenario has the makings of a hell of a B-grade movie, complete with drifting mist, disembodied voices and wet footsteps leading to the edge of cliff. Remember *The Fog*—that John Carpenter movie about the radio station in an old lighthouse and the shipwrecks whose victims terrorize the sleepy town of Antonio Bay when the fog creeps in from the sea?

A lighthouse in the fog: the ideal setting for strange happenings.

Or maybe you've read Frank Parker Day's classic novel *Rockbound*, where the keeper of the light on Barren Island (modelled after Pearl Island, near Nova Scotia's Mahone Bay) endures wicked storms and the cries and pleas of restless spirits. Throughout a long, rum-soaked night, the keeper and his companion entertain each other on this "rare night for ghosts." Twice the men spring to their feet and fly to the lantern at the horrendous sound of shattering glass. But the lamp burns steady despite the tempest without and the spirits within.

"No sleep for us tonight, lad," says the keeper. "One o' dem minor haunts is workin' on us."

I'm getting shivery just thinking about it. Or maybe it's just that half-empty quart bottle of Demerara rum at my elbow.

I don't know if there are more lighthouse ghost stories per capita than just the run-of-the-mill mainland hauntings or happenings, but as soon as you mention living at a lighthouse, someone is bound to ask "Did you ever have any strange experiences out there?"

If you have a mind that runs to such things, then it's pretty fair to say that you'll see or hear something at a lighthouse. After hearing a couple of ghost stories from George Locke on Cross Island—one of them quite startling—my mind got working a bit. I was vigilant for ghosts as I drove the tractor along the dark lighthouse road to check the boat on stormy nights.

On one occasion, I carefully poked my head through the attic hatch of the next-door house when a frightened relief keeper declared that someone—no, something!—was slowly walking above the ceiling. Of course there was no one there—in the cool of the night after a hot and sultry day, the wooden beams and rafters were contracting, creaking and groaning a bit. We turned our attention back to the television.

The biggest fright I ever got came when I was alone on the island. The fiery red sun was just preparing to dip into the sea and the crows were wheeling and cawing over the spruces, getting ready to settle for the night. I had climbed the lighthouse—a hollow fibreglass tower with a ladder attached to the inside for access to the lantern—to stand on the lantern deck, smell the sea, and enjoy the fading moments of daylight.

Ducking in through the lantern door, I slowly climbed back down the ladder. As I reached the concrete floor at the bottom of the tower, I froze. I could feel something behind me. Almost like a breath on my neck, the sense was tangible. As the grit below my feet crackled, I felt it again—hands reaching out to touch me.

I whipped around, and there it was!

Nothing.

All I'd felt and heard was the sound of my feet reflected by the concave walls of the tower behind me. Like one of those parabolic whisper reflectors in a kids' science centre. Heart pounding and sheepish, I stepped out and closed the door.

It was a pretty prosaic outcome to what could have been an interesting interlude, but I'm certainly not saying that all strange experiences are the result of an overactive imagination. Some just happen out of the blue.

When my friend Rip Irwin was in the middle of his quest to visit every lighthouse in Nova Scotia, he found himself storm-stayed on Guyon Island for a few days. Just off the east coast of Cape Breton near Gabarus, the island has a reputation as a bad place. Rip, a no-nonsense former Navy Chief Petty Officer, found himself increasingly uncomfortable as he huddled in one of the abandoned keepers' houses, waiting for the wind to let up.

It was nothing he could pin a name to—just a feeling that he wasn't welcome on the island. The wind, slashing rain, and derelict houses didn't do much to make Guyon a happy place during Rip's visit, but there was more to it than the weather.

After six days he finally got off the island. Rip later found out that the island had a history of funny goings on, including a series of "strange happenings and noises…occurring with such regularity that the RCMP was brought to the island to investigate."

The last keepers left Guyon in 1986, and unless someone else is marooned on the island, no one will ever know exactly what makes the island an uncomfortable place to visit. The same is true of the rest of Nova Scotia's keeperless lights, but the stories live on—as evocative as the wind whistling through the cracked windows of an abandoned lighthouse—in the memories of the people who came face-to-face with the unexpected.

DOUBLE ALEC—SAMBRO ISLAND'S SPECTRE

One of Nova Scotia's most enduring lighthouse ghost stories involves Sambro Island. Well suited for a haunting, it's a desolate spot—a small granite mound, topped with a bit of wind-blasted grass and scrub at the southwestern approaches to Halifax Harbour. Part of a series of treacherous ledges, the island was an ideal spot for a lighthouse to guard the harbour entrance. A scant nine years after the founding of the garrison town of Halifax in 1749, the colonial government of the day began construction of a stone tower on the island for precisely that purpose. Workers completed the fortress-like tower with its thick granite walls and gun-slit windows in early 1760.

The Sambro Island light as it appeared during Double Alec's time.

Lightkeeper Joseph Rous, who had arrived on the island in 1759 to keep a temporary light, subsequently turned his attention to maintaining the smoky fish oil-burning lamps that helped guide shipping into the harbour.

The area's frequent fogs proved to be a problem for vessels trying to feel their way into the harbour and, even worse, through the surrounding ledges. By the late 1790s, the government posted members of the Royal Artillery to the island to maintain a signal station, to help vessels navigate through the blinding white fog.

Artillerymen continued to live on the island until 1888, when they abandoned their cannons and left Sambro to the lightkeeper and his family. And a ghost named Double Alec.

Local legend has it that Alex Alexander (hence the nickname) was one of the four members of the Royal Artillery posted to the island in the 1870s. Alex (known locally as "Alec") was apparently a free-thinking artilleryman. Entrusted with money for supplies, he went ashore one day only to drink the money away, or spend it at local house of ill-repute, or both (depending on who you talk to).

According to Minnie Smith—whose grandfather, William Gilkie, was the lightkeeper at the time—Alec was gone for a week, and returned to the island broke, hung over and remorseful.

"Alec wanted the captain, the head fellow of the army, to give him a drink of rum to straighten him out. The captain wouldn't do it. So then Alec went and hung himself. He hung himself in the whistle house. Whoever found him came running down and said to my grandfather, 'Grandfather come quick, Alec hung himself.' The head fellow went up and they cut him down and he still was warm and he still had a heartbeat. My grandfather said to him, 'Do you have a penknife on you?' to draw out a little bit of blood on him. 'The veins will start going and his heart will come back.'

"The captain said, 'No, it's not allowed in the British Army.' So they let Alec die. He could have been saved, but they let him go."

Minnie told me that not long after Alec died, strange things began to happen on the island. "My grandfather, he had one of those big Newfoundland dogs. It was comin' up a storm one night and he said to my grandmother, 'Mary, I'll go down and check the boats, for it's going to be a storm.' So he went to the back cove with the dog and there was Alec. Grandfather called his dog and the dog wouldn't go. Alec was just there for a minute or so, and then he just disappeared."

Not every keeper on Sambro Island experienced Double Alec, but one family more than made up for the ghost-free years following William Gilkie's face-to-face meeting with the spectre. John and Marjorie Fairservice were the last keepers on Sambro. Between 1964 and 1988 they raised a family of three kids on the island. They also met up with Alec on more than one occasion.

Just before the family came ashore for good in March 1988, I spent a couple of nights at the light with the Fairservices, my friend Rip Irwin, and a relief keeper. One evening, we all crowded into John and

Marjorie's small living room. Outside it was blowing a gale, buffeting the house as the foghorn rattled the windows.

Inside, through a haze of cigarette smoke, John, Marjorie and their daughter Kelly told us of their experiences with Double Alec: the toilet that occasionally flushed by itself, the footsteps upstairs when the house was empty, the dark figure of a man on the beach when there was no one else on the island. One visitor to the Fairservices declared to John that there was a third man in the kitchen with them, dressed in a British uniform "from the olden days."

The skeptic might say well, so what? Those are just stories and how can you prove it was Alec, or anything? Well, you can't. But just ask Kelly about the night Alec tried to get in bed with a friend of hers.

It was back in the mid-1980s. Kelly was working in the offshore oil industry and she'd brought a friend, Vicki, who also worked on the rigs, back home for a visit. They were with the family in the living room watching a movie when Vicki decided to turn in for the night.

She was soon back downstairs, however, snuggling up close to Kelly on the couch. But it wasn't until the safety of the light of day that Vicki haltingly explained to Kelly what had happened.

"She said she was almost asleep," Kelly told me, "and that she thought it was me coming to bed because she felt somebody sit down on the edge of the bed. The covers went back and then she felt this big pressure, like somebody laid right on top of her."

But there was no one in the room. Terrified, Vicki pushed back the covers and stumbled downstairs to the warmth and light of the crowd in the living room. Kelly hadn't told her friend the stories about Double Alec beforehand, and she wasn't "the nervous type." But the brief meeting in bed with Alec made a lasting impression on Vicki, although to this day, no one knows what *really* happened that night on Sambro Island.

HORATIO NELSON'S GHOST

Double Alec has definitely scared a few people, but he's just the spirit of a lowly artilleryman. Farther down the eastern shore, on Kent Island, there lurks a much more imposing presence—the ghost of the storied British admiral, Horatio Nelson.

These tranquil shores are also home to the Kents—Ivan is the fourth generation of his family to live in the Kent homestead on Pleasant Point, just east of Musquodoboit Harbour. Back in 1904 the department of Marine and Fisheries built a set of range lights to guide shipping into safe anchorage. John Kent kept the rear light at Pleasant Point and later passed his duties to his son and grandson, until the light was automated in 1951.

Ivan grew up helping his father and mother tend the light, and along the way he also learned of his family's history. His great grandfather was a "man o' war," in the British navy, serving under Nelson and then retiring to live out his days on a two-thousand-acre grant in Nova

Ivan Kent and the lighthouse haunted by the spirit of Admiral Horatio Nelson

Scotia. According to Ivan, his great-grandfather always claimed there was a ghost in his house when he built it, but he forbade anyone to speak of the spectre.

Ruddy faced and slow spoken, Ivan took up the story during my visit with him and his wife Mildred on a brilliant September day in 2001.

"In 1903, they tore the old house down and built the lighthouse," Ivan told me. "Of course the ghost showed up in the lighthouse, which was a natural state of affairs. But we never knew who the ghost was.

"We've had a lot of people here over the years that will go over there not knowin' anything about a ghost in the lighthouse and they'll come back and the first question they'll ask me is, 'Is there a ghost in that lighthouse?' One couple, as soon as they went in they said they could feel a presence there. Another couple claimed they could feel something *around* the lighthouse."

But it wasn't until a group of visitors came to stay with Ivan and Mildred at their bed and breakfast that the story of the lighthouse haunting began to take shape.

"An old German lady come here from New York City with two of her nieces. One girl was from Switzerland and she didn't know any English at all. The other girl knew sixteen languages and she had a license to teach thirteen languages and was still goin' to university!

"She wanted to go out the lighthouse that evening. It was gettin' quite twilight and I didn't like anyone goin' over there alone that late in the evening. But she persistently wanted to go that night so I said, 'Well alright, I'll go along with you.'"

As Ivan and the young visitor walked to the lighthouse, he told her about some of the strange incidents over the years. After finding out that there was a spirit in the lighthouse, the young woman lit up, saying "I'm so happy there's a ghost there! I've had several encounters with ghosts."

It turned out she could tell fortunes as well and she read Ivan's hand. "She told me my life story better than I could remember it myself," he said, grimacing. "She could tell ya things in so much detail that I was gettin' a little worried that she may know some things I'd rather she didn't!"

A month or two later the Kents had a letter from the fortune teller, who had made it her business to find out just who the ghost in the tower was. It was, she wrote "that great British Admiral, Lord Horatio Nelson!"

Ivan continued. "Well now, we kind of smiled at that at first, but when I looked back at the history of my family, my great-grandfather had sailed with Admiral Nelson for several years. He was his navigating officer on the *Victory* and he went through the battle of the Nile in 1798 and he was with him at Trafalgar in 1805, when Nelson was killed."

Ivan's theory, related with a half-smile, was that Nelson decided to tag along with his former navigating officer (and Ivan's great-grandfather) to Nova Scotia. Better than being buried all alone in London!

"I suppose his spirit thought to himself, 'What the hell's the point of me goin' up there to London with that miserable body? It's only got one eye and one arm anyway. So, here's my navigating officer, he's been with me for a long time and he'll be goin' to sea for a long time yet. I'll stay aboard with him!'

"So he sailed with my great grandfather the rest of his career. When great grandfather retired he was based here in Halifax after 1808, and for the last four years he served, he was governor of the Melville Island prison on the Northwest Arm in Halifax. When he retired and he got this grant of land, he come down here and built his house. Nelson moved in with him!

"I think the old fella knew who the ghost was and that's why he discouraged people from talkin' about it. After all he didn't want his revered old admiral and commanding officer talked about like he was a ghost!"

Ivan enjoyed playing up the story. He even went so far as to put a picnic table on the hill near the lighthouse. When he and Mildred operated their B&B, he instructed their guests not to use the table after ten at night.

"That's reserved for them two old fellers to have a yarn out there on the hill, which I expect they do on them stormy nights," he'd say. "A great place for them to have their tot of rum!"

FORERUNNERS AND COLD FIRE

We seem to be at the end of the era of folklore and oral tradition. Even in quaint little Nova Scotia, so tied to the sea, with our ruddy-cheeked fishermen and our simple, honest ways—okay, that's the tourism spiel, but there's a germ of truth there—we're pretty wrapped up in big-box shopping, the information highway, and getting to and from wherever we're going or coming as fast as possible.

There doesn't seem to be much room for the old stories anymore—that cultural heritage we used to share around the fire and pass from generation to generation. Ghost stories have become light fare for entertainment's sake, instead of a way of explaining unexplainable things.

But it wasn't so long ago that ghosts, forerunners and bumps in the night were an accepted part of every day life, especially in isolated communities. Beginning in the 1930s, folklorist Helen Creighton made it her mission to collect some of this heritage, in the form of songs and stories sung and told by the people of rural Nova Scotia.

Creighton spent much of her time on Devil's Island, a flat, treeless oval just a stone's throw from Hartlen Point on the Dartmouth side of Halifax Harbour. The island was home to more than a dozen fishing families until the 1940s, when the last stragglers moved ashore to a more modern life on the main.

Perhaps because of its island status, oral tradition throve on Devil's Island, as did beliefs in the old ways of superstition. Ina (Henneberry) York was born on the island in 1925. She left in the 1940s after marrying her sweetheart, Clyde York, and settling in nearby Eastern Passage. I interviewed Ina in her apartment in Cole Harbour, in the midst of fast-food joints and strip malls. It seemed like an incongruous setting for stories of forerunners and strange happenings, but Ina still believed what she had seen and heard on Devil's Island.

"My cousin drowned takin' some fellas over to the lower end of Eastern Passage," she told me. "He took them over and he never come back. We waited and waited and waited. He still never come back. And then we looked out the window and we saw him walkin' up to the house. But he never come in the house, so they went lookin' for him.

"My other cousin, he went lookin' for him in his boat and he said he felt somethin' grab on to the stern of the flat [boat], but he didn't get in the boat. They went draggin' for him the next day and my Dad got [his body]."

Then there was the case of the cold fire. Helen Creighton makes note of this Devil's Island phenomenon in *Bluenose Ghosts*, describing a particular house that would catch fire, but remain cool enough that you could put your hand on the shingles. Ina remembered a similar incident at the old house.

"Aunt Alice's house caught on fire—the roof. That house was supposed to be the ghost house—and Andy Edwards got up on the ladder. They started formin' a bucket brigade from the well. Andy got up to throw the water on, and after the first bucket of water he threw, he said, 'Don't bother bringin' any more.' He put his hand right in the fire. He said, 'The fire is cold.' And with that the fire died down."

Ina looked at her husband and then at me. "I was there! I saw that!"

In the background, Clyde snorted and said "All imagination!"

"Well, we all had a good imagination, then," Ina countered. "People were very, very superstitious!"

She continued. "I, myself, had a forerunner. Florence Faulkner was my very best friend, and she was sick in the hospital. Her brother Ken, he was the lighthouse keeper. One day he was gone in town to the hospital. This was the start of the war, and at a certain time each day, like three o'clock and seven o'clock you had to listen on the radio. They would say 'A for Apple' if everything was fine, 'B for Butter' if there was a warning—that meant put the light out, there's submarine out there—and 'C for Charlie': the coast is clear."

"So I went back over a little before three, turned the radio on, and listened. I got the 'A for Apple,' and I was just ready to leave when I heard BANG! upstairs. I said 'Uh-oh, must be window open. I heard a door slam.' I went upstairs and every room door was open and every window was closed. So I went downstairs again. Just got down there when I heard the same thing. BANG! It happened *three* times. The third time I didn't go back up!

"When Ken come home he said 'Florence died at three o'clock.'"

Ina looked at me quizzically. "So what would you call that? Another one of them ghost stories? But that was true, that one!"

BONES FOR UNCLE FRANK

Tales of ghosts and strange happenings take on a life of their own, sometimes evolving from simple events. This next story doesn't really concern the supernatural, but it's the kind of tale that in a century's time could evolve into something much more macabre. It was macabre enough for Ina York's parents.

"We had a little stove in the parlour, a round stove," Ina told me. "We used to call it Uncle Frank, 'cause Mum had bought it from Frank deYoung. When she would make a barley soup, with those big beef bones, she'd always throw the bone in Uncle Frank and burn it up."

But a stove can't heat a house on bones alone. Devil's had long since lost its trees, and with up to sixteen families living on the island, it was an important task to gather wood for hungry stoves. Ina and her sister would often tag along with their parents to gather fuel on nearby Thrumcap, at the southern tip of McNabs Island.

"I was about eight years old and my older sister about ten. Mum and Dad and we two kids went over to Thrumcap to gather up bags of wood. Now when we'd go, we'd have a lot of bags together. Mum and Dad was back there gatherin'—we were over here gatherin'—and we found all those bones. So I said, 'Joan, let's gather up some bones for Uncle Frank.' So we took two bags—one each—and we filled them with those bones.

"When we were comin' home, I said 'Dad, have we got a surprise for you and Mum! We got two bags of bones for Uncle Frank!'

"Well, Dad was too dark," Ina chuckled as she remembered the day. "He couldn't turn white, but Mum did! Dad took the bags and he undid the strings and he dumped them over the side. He said, 'The water from

Joan and Ina Henneberry show some style at Devil's Island around 1940.

the storms washes down and them are all graves in there and them bones are from the people that was buried in there!'

"So we had two bags of human bones to take home to burn! They got a watery grave before we got home, though!"

SOMETHING'S WATCHING US

Even Ina York, living in the thick of forerunners and cold fires on Devil's Island, didn't have the sheer concentrated spectral experiences of the Locke family.

The Lockes with their Country Island neighbours, Ardath and Vernon Zwicker.

George and Ethel Locke raised their three kids—Daniel, Denise and Sandra—on four islands along the eastern and southern shores of Nova Scotia. George had been a career fisherman until losing his boat to fire. In 1975 he opted for a more secure (if less lucrative) job as a lightkeeper, so the family could be together. Plus, as he told me, "the islands didn't rock and roll!"

After a year and a half on tiny Flint Island, near Port Morien, Cape Breton, George transferred to the larger Country Island, where there was room to roam and even keep a few animals. The kids liked their new home, playing outside on the barren lighthouse grounds and amongst the stunted spruces.

But when the day waned, that was it. Not one of them would stay outside, no matter how warm or pleasant the evening. Daniel Locke was about eight at the time, and he still clearly remembers the feeling.

"It was always like someone was watchin' you, or someone was walkin' behind you," he told me. "We'd never go outside at night. If we had to walk down the engine room with Dad in the night we'd be so close to his rear end that we were almost in his back pocket!"

That feeling of being watched wasn't limited to the kids. George didn't like the way his neck prickled as he walked down the long boardwalk from his house to the engine room in the wee hours of the morning.

"To tell you the truth I was never comfortable on Country Island," he said with a shake of his head. "I'll tell you, at two o'clock in the morning, walkin' down that boardwalk, it was a long walk! It was just the same as if somebody was walking along behind you. The dog would feel it too. I'd like to know how many times the dog would run ahead of me and stop, and the old hair would come up on its back and it would growl. No way could you coax that dog to go down that boardwalk any farther!"

There were other strange things too. Someone or something regularly moved the top of the well off during the night. The next day it would take the two keepers to put it back in place. What's more, something or someone enjoyed scattering the head keeper's tools all over the boathouse, and it wasn't the kids because they wouldn't dare set foot outdoors at night!

One of the most disturbing episodes happened just after George and Ethel moved onto the island in 1977. At three o'clock in the morning, Ethel awoke from a sound sleep to a clattering in the basement. Thinking it was Vernon, the head keeper, coming to let George know about a problem with the equipment, she didn't worry as footsteps came up the basements steps and shuffled across the hallway's hardwood floors. The steps continued past Ethel's bedroom door and on to the next two rooms.

By this time Ethel was a little nervous, as she hadn't heard anyone speak. She was too scared to call out, and lay huddled in bed as the footsteps came slowly back down the hall, paused outside her door, then creaked through the kitchen and into the basement again.

By the light of day Ethel thought little of her nocturnal visitor, until she asked Vernon why he'd been in the house in the early hours of the morning.

Barren Country Island— there's nowhere for peeping toms to hide, but the Lockes felt like they were continually being "watched."

But Vernon had been asleep in his own bed, in his own house.

There were other incidents—the sounds of pipes crashing to the floor in the basement, and more hackles-raising encounters for the dog, but until the Lockes moved down the shore to White Head Island in 1979, they learned to live with the Country Island's restless presence.

HOLY JESUS!
YOU SAW OLD JIM BURGOYNE!

There was a two-year lull in the Lockes' mysterious experiences while they lived on White Head Island, in Guysborough County. Windy, foggy, granite-bound, and cold, the island was "so desolate a ghost wouldn't stay on it," as George told me.

But then came a transfer to Cross Island.

Sitting in the broad mouth of Lunenburg Harbour, the island was a pastoral paradise compared to the Lockes' previous three postings. The lighthouse, although exposed to summer's southwest winds and fog, sat on a mowed patch amidst a lush field of tall grass. Along the east side, a road of crushed shale meandered along the sharp cliffs and through spruce trees to the landing on the north end.

There was a chance to do a little fishing and keep a garden. George and young Daniel enjoyed duck and deer hunting, and there were lots of visitors on hot summer weekends—a perfect time to raft up in one of the islands' shale-armed inlets and shoot the breeze.

But it wasn't long before another type of visitor came to call.

It was about suppertime on a clear summer's day. George and Daniel were across the harbour on the north end of the island, working on the station boat, which they'd hauled up on the slip. George looked up to see Ethel on the opposite side of the harbour and told Daniel, "Go over and pick your mother up. Tell her I'll be another hour, and we'll all go home together."

Daniel jumped in the skiff and started to row over. About halfway over he stopped for a moment or two, and continued on. As he beached the skiff on the grey shale beach his mother asked him, "Smitty have any fish?"

"Smitty" was the nickname for Earl Smith, a retired keeper who still kept a camp on the island. He often came out to handline and spend a night or two in the harbour. Young Daniel looked confused. "Smitty's not down," he said.

Ethel looked at her son strangely. "He was just up alongside you, and he stopped to talk to you," she said.

"Smitty ain't down, Mum!" Daniel repeated.

By this time Ethel was getting annoyed at Daniel for pulling her leg. She'd seen a white boat come in through the gut near the boat slip, and she'd seen it stop alongside her son's skiff. The little bugger was lying!

Daniel stuck to his guns, even rowing his mother up to Smitty's camp to show her that his boat was not there. At the slipway, Ethel asked George about the white boat that had come through the gut. George hadn't seen the boat. Ethel was sure her husband and son were just giving her the gears.

Summer gave way to cool nights and autumn winds and Ethel was left to ponder what she had seen. But not for long. Late in the fall, Ethel decided to walk to the landing and wait for George as he worked aboard the station boat, at anchor in the harbour. Once again, a small, white, open boat with a lone figure came in through the gut, stopping next to George and the station boat. Thinking it was Smitty, Ethel decided to walk back to the light, as George would likely want to have a yarn with the old gent.

On the way back to the light Ethel was surprised when George pulled up behind her in the tractor. "You weren't talking to Smitty very long," she said.

"Smitty ain't down!" George replied, confused.

"George, don't lie to me! I saw him come in the harbour," Ethel said. By this time, she was getting annoyed. But to prove it, George took his wife back over the beach and they rowed over to Smitty's camp.

No boat. No Smitty.

A few days later the flesh-and-blood Smitty and his wife Rita came out to spend a few days at their camp. Time to set the record straight. After all, Ethel had seen a white boat, twice, with a man in it.

Until the day she died, Ethel Locke's voice would crack when she told the story of seeing old Jim Burgoyne at the tiller of his ghost craft.

She explained what the boat looked like—small, white, with a mast and a man at the tiller. What did it sound like? Like a putt-putt. An old make-and-break.

Rita Smith shot Ethel a look and turned as white as a ghost. Her husband said, "Holy Jesus. You saw old Jim Burgoyne. He was a lobster fisherman drowned off the Hounds ledges years ago. When he fished off here, he'd stand back with the tiller in his hand and come up the harbour. I can still see him."

Ethel died in 1990, but to the end of her days, her voice would crack when she told the story. She'd seen that old boat twice, with the ghost of Jim Burgoyne at the tiller, even if everyone else thought she was crazy.

In the summer of 2004, a family friend vindicated Ethel's claims. One day, he came over to shake her son's hand during a visit to the island. Daniel looked surprised. "I finally seen him," the friend said. Then he explained. That week, he and his wife had seen the white boat with the mast and the putt-putt and the man at the tiller, right up in the harbour. The couple looked at each other, shocked. Turning their heads back again, they looked for the white boat and the man at the tiller.

It was gone.

IT WAS A FACE YOU'D NEVER FORGET

Even though Ethel Locke swore she saw a man who had been dead and gone many years, her family remained skeptical. After all, no one else had seen anything strange. At least, not until one night in the mid-1980s.

George and a friend of the family had walked to the harbour to check the station boat. Young Daniel, in his early teens, was already an old hand on the tractor and he had permission to drive over to meet the men.

It was a beautiful, calm night. Daniel backed the old tractor out of the garage and eased it down the hill. On one side, dark spruce trees hemmed the narrow road, and on the other, scrub and shale parted occasionally to reveal the sea lapping along narrow inlets. Ahead, the trees grew on both sides, forming a dark tunnel. A good place for a smoke!

Daniel slowed the tractor, keeping it in gear but depressing the clutch. Bending his neck towards a flaring match, he lit a cigarette—and looked up.

In front of him stood a man.

Daniel stared. The figure, only an engine bonnet away, glowed white.

"He had a fisherman's knit sweater on," Daniel remembered twenty years later. "I can still see it to this day, the pattern with the diamond shapes. It was an off-white colour. He had a grey-brown beard. I remember that. And he had one of those hats you wear on the side, like a tam. He had chubby cheeks. I remember it the same as if it was yesterday."

Head cocked to one side, the man looked at Daniel. For a split second, Daniel stared back. Then he screamed and popped the clutch. The tractor lurched down the dark trail, Daniel hollering at the top of his lungs.

"Every time the mud would fly off the tractor wheels and show up in the headlights, 'Aaahhhh!'—I'd holler again!"

Wide-eyed and trembling, Daniel arrived at the harbour, where his father ran to see what the hell was wrong. When Daniel had stuttered his story, George said, "Jesus Christ, someone probably got shipwrecked and you ran them over!"

So they all drove back to the spot. No footprints. No sign of anyone. Just the spun-up gravel from the tractor's panicked wheels.

It took a while for Daniel to get over the shock of seeing the glowing man in front of his headlights. "If I was by myself hunting I was always past that spot long before dark. Even today, I'm past that spot before dark."

Daniel Locke is not a fellow to spook easily—he's been a scallop fisherman, and he now works as a mate on an offshore supply vessel, spending his shifts in Cameroon, Angola, Greece. Places a lot more dangerous than Cross Island.

But Daniel told me he'd like to see the man again. "He'd scare me for a second or two, but I'd like to find out what his problem is! Maybe he needs someone to pray for him!"

He paused for a moment. "I can still see him now, just like it's twenty years ago," he said quietly. "It's a face you'd never forget."

The lighthouse road, where Daniel Locke ran his tractor "through" a man, is now almost overgrown.

9

War

IN PEACE TIME, CANADIAN LIGHTHOUSES AND THEIR KEEPERS were vital to the protection of mariners against the dangers of darkness and storm. In times of war, lighthouses were doubly important, guarding not only against the vagaries of weather, but the threat of enemy attack.

As the only government presence—and only points of civilization—along thousands of kilometres of a mostly dark and thinly populated coastline, lighthouses were a natural choice for involvement in the Canadian government's coastal observation system.

During World War Two, many lighthouses in Nova Scotia became part of the Aircraft Detection Corps, with their keepers (and family members) acting as the ears and eyes of a government increasingly concerned by enemy action in *our* waters. But the very attributes that made lighthouses well-suited to assist in coastal defence—vantage, elevation and round-the-clock observers—also meant they were vulnerable to attack.

Fortunately, with one notable exception, no Canadian lighthouses were ever directly attacked during World War Two. Lighthouses and foghorns were as useful to enemy vessels and aircraft as friendly ships, which might explain why no Nova Scotia lights were ever shelled or bombed.

This was not the case in British Columbia, where at Estevan Point "the quiet lighthouse life was shattered" on the evening

The Navy-run radar tower at Duncan's Cove, near Chebucto Head Lighthouse.

of June 20, 1942. Official accounts later revealed that Japanese submarine I-26 had surfaced off the isolated point on the west coast of Vancouver Island, firing twenty-five five-inch shells at the station. "Estevan Point," notes author Donald Graham in his book *Keepers of the Light*, "went down in history as the first place where enemy shells had struck Canadian soil since [the war of] 1812."

Running up the tower to extinguish the light inside the massive first-order Fresnel lens, lightkeeper Robert Lally watched the barrage from the balcony of his thirty-metre tall concrete monolith. Some of the shells landed short of the lightstation; others passed overhead, landing in the forest beyond. Lally ran down the tower to safety.

When it was all over, there were no injuries on the station—just a few shaken residents and some smashed glass in the lantern. But to this day, controversy surrounds the shelling of Estevan Point. Some speculate that it wasn't a Japanese sub that shelled Estevan Point at all, but an American vessel, as part of a covert operation to unite Canadians behind the war effort (especially given Prime Minister William Lyon Mackenzie King's "long-standing promise to avoid conscription").

No matter who fired the shells, that attack on Estevan Point showed that war *could* come to us as well. Fortunately, Canadian lightkeepers were lucky—their brethren in the United Kingdom and Europe were often in the thick of it.

Half a year before shells sent the occupants of Estevan Point running for cover, the wife of an assistant keeper at Fair Isle South in Scotland's Shetland Islands was killed and her infant daughter hurt during an air attack.

And on January 21, 1942, the wife and daughter of the principal lightkeeper died when a second air attack smashed the main dwelling in the late afternoon. Assistant keeper Roderick Macaulay struggled three miles through snowdrifts and gale-force winds from the island's other lighthouse to help get the south light up and running again, as the shattered station buildings around it burned. Macaulay had lived through his own nightmare just a short time before, when he and his daughter narrowly escaped a previous air raid.

Still, Nova Scotia's lightkeepers and their families weren't far from the action. In her book *B Was For Butter*, Evelyn Richardson writes of hearing the sounds of fighting at sea.

> As well as explosions from what we judged to be torpedoes, we often heard the booms of heavier guns than those carried by U-boats. Often the force of depth-charges, transmitted through the water, shook the Point's bedrock while, indoors, the lighthouse walls trembled, floors wavered and windows rattled. At these time we could picture our surface craft and planes attacking enemy wolf packs.

The crew of the Sambro Lightship, off Halifax Harbour, was even closer to the action. Although German U-boats never tried to sink the lightship—it was too useful for their own operations—the Canadian minesweeper *Clayoquot* sank after a torpedo ripped through its hull on Christmas Eve in 1944, just five miles away from the lightship. In April 1945, torpedoes pierced the minesweeper *Esquimalt* in sight of the *Sambro Lightship*, sending the vessel to the bottom along with many of its crew.

War changed lightkeeping in Nova Scotia. What was already a labour-intensive, relentless affair was now even more involved and risky. Added responsibilities, such as listening for regular radio instructions regarding the operation of lights and horns, made keepers virtual slaves to the clock. Aircraft Detection Corps work meant that planes had to be identified, logged and regularly reported to the Department of Transport.

As Fiona Marshall writes in her master's thesis on the life and work of Evelyn Richardson, the World War Two years represented "the height of importance for the lightkeeping service." For an intense period between 1939 and 1945, Nova Scotia lightkeepers played a crucial role in defending not only "their family, community, island, coastline and province, but their fellow Canadians as well."

THE ABCS OF COASTAL DEFENCE

The 1930s saw a slowly gathering storm spread dark clouds across Europe. At the beginning of the decade, Adolf Hitler's National Socialist Party (commonly called the Nazi Party) was the second largest political entity in Germany. By the summer of 1934, the Nazis were declared the *only* party in the country, just weeks after the opening of the Dachau concentration camp.

Introducing military conscription and stripping German Jews of their rights, Hitler—as *fuhrer* of a totalitarian state—had free reign to exert his terrifying power over a widening base. By 1936 German troops occupied the Rhineland. Over the next three years Germany's territorial demands grew, troops occupied the Sudentanland and the Czech government resigned.

Finally, on September 1, 1939, Germany invaded Poland. Two days later Britain, France, Australia, and New Zealand declared war on Germany. A week later Canada followed suit, and the Battle of the Atlantic began, plunging the world into more than five years of tumult and terror.

In November, the war arrived officially at Nova Scotia's lightstations, as keepers became part of the coastal defence system. The Department of Transport provided lighkeepers with a coded set of instructions, which for the duration of the conflict would control how and when their lights and horns were to be operated.

It would also make keepers a slave to their clocks, after generations of living by the rules of wind, tide, fog and the hours of sun-up and sun-down. Now the clock was king. Every four hours, the strident notes of "Rule Britannia," broadcast from radio station CBA in Sackville, New Brunswick, preceded coded instructions from the government.

These directives came to Bon Portage Island on November 13, when Morrill Richardson had picked up the mail in Shag Harbour. The message from the area marine agent was brief: "Enclosed are instructions which you are to follow out carefully. They are to be kept locked up and divulged to no one."

Then came the details:

INSTRUCTION "A"- Navigational lights are to be exhibited
and fog signals and radio beacons operated normally.

INSTRUCTION "B"- Extinguish navigational lights and cease
operating fog signals and radio beacons until further orders.

INSTRUCTION "C"- Cancel Instruction "B". Lights are to be
exhibited and fog signals and radio beacons operated normally.

Today, the code—A for Apples, B for Butter and C for Charlie—
seems ridiculously simple. But I have talked with keepers' kids who to
this day don't know what it all meant.

Certainly at the time, no one other than lightkeepers knew the
code—with at least one exception. Bon Portage, although an offshore
lighthouse, only had one keeper. This situation made it necessary for
Morrill to share the top secret code with his wife Evelyn (with the
government's permission).

The radio schedule became Evelyn's almost exclusively, as Morrill
was often working outside the lighthouse. When work took the whole
family outside, Evelyn brought the alarm clock along to remind her
of the next broadcast. Even at home in the lighthouse, as Evelyn later
wrote, the routine was wearisome.

"The only time either Morrill or I knew an uninterrupted night's
sleep was when one of us was ill and the other doing double duty."
During the winter months there were added challenges. It wasn't safe to
keep a fire burning through the night, and the Richardsons did not want
to trust themselves to keep the radio near a warm bed, where there was
no guarantee that they'd stay awake for the required listening period.

So, as the jangling alarm signaled the 3:30 A.M. listening period in
the dead of a bitter winter night, Evelyn wrote that they "struggled out
of bed to spend five to ten minutes in agonized sleepiness and shivering
discomfort in the drafty living room, where...the wind was always
rattling the windows in their shrunken sashes and shrieking about

the metal lantern. It was a lonely vigil…and…a time when imagined dangers from a lurking enemy caused grave concern for our children sleeping upstairs."

Then, the now familiar strains of "Rule Britannia," followed by: "Attention lightkeepers. All lightkeepers in East Coast areas. Instructions A—A for Apples—is to be carried out."

After a sigh of relief, Evelyn could crawl back to bed for a blessed, short sleep until the next listening schedule.

For the Richardsons, instruction "A" gave some measure of comfort in troubling times. But that changed on the afternoon of May 31, 1940. As a "sullen spring fog driven by a cold sea wind," enveloped the island, the announcer on the radio spoke: "Message for Lightkeepers in Area 2. Carry out Instructions B, B for Butter."

Evelyn ran off to find Morrill, realizing at once "how vulnerable and defenseless was our lighthouse, facing any seaborn enemy." The Richardsons spent an anxious couple of hours by the radio, listening for further instructions. Finally, the welcome "C, C for Charlie" came through the speaker, allowing the keepers to heave a sigh of relief and return to their duties.

Later, Evelyn learned that on the same day a notice had flashed across the screen in a movie house in Yarmouth, ordering all servicemen to report to their stations. A man who had served in the military later told Evelyn "that was the time we were issued live ammunition and told to shoot to kill." Richardson did not say if any soldier did in fact "shoot to kill," but later wrote that she believed the "B" message had been a test of lightkeepers' readiness.

AIRCRAFT DETECTION CORPS

By 1942, with the war in full swing, life continued to get busier for Nova Scotia's keepers. In January, Eastern Air Command sent out a set of instructions to lightstations detailing new duties for "Official Observers." It was a serious business—keepers filled out "declaration

The Standard

10 CENTS

PHOTONEWS

JUNE 20 1942

OFFICIAL OBSERVER

LIGHTHOUSE KEEPER Eddie Gallagher, silhouetted in hard, warily studies approaching planes. Somewhere Along Atlantic Coast" Corps of War-watchers help to protect the country against surprise Axis attacks.

Edward Gallagher scans the sky for aircraft at Chebucto Head, near Halifax, in 1942.

of secrecy forms" and were forbidden to talk with other civilians about their responsibilities.

Keepers now had to log sightings of aircraft, submarines and surface craft. They were also cautioned to keep a sharp eye out for everything from strange lights or signals, "persons attempting to rent small boats to go off to sea," and even "any unusual camping ground on or near the coast.

Most importantly, if you did spot anything out of the ordinary, you were to "Report Exactly as Follows: By TELEPHONE, TELEGRAPH or WIRELESS—AND DO IT FAST."

This was not necessarily an easy task if you didn't have communications with the mainland. Bon Portage Island had no telephone and no two-way radio, so any reports would have to be phoned from the mainland, assuming the weather would allow the lightkeeper to leave the island in the first place.

The marine agent even went as far as to request Morrill Richardson "investigate" the Ardnamurchan Club in nearby Argyle. The agent explained that all clubs and organizations that might be fronts for enemy agents had to be checked out. "Just how the Department," Evelyn Richardson wrote, "expected Morrill, on 24-hour duty and with no car to investigate a mainland club some thirty miles away, was not explained."

The department also issued keepers with submarine report forms. German U-boats were exacting a heavy toll on Allied vessels and torpedoing fishing boats, and the disturbing site of a conning tower rising above the sea was not rare. "Sometimes it was an uneasy feeling out there," said Kay Ingersoll of the war years on Gannet Rock. "We always saw the convoys going out of Saint John, out into the bay and crossing the Atlantic. You just had a feeling maybe there were some people lurking around there underwater that perhaps you didn't know about."

Gannet Rock's keepers were no strangers to war and submarines. Kay remembered her mother telling her about a boat that was torpedoed by a submarine near the Murr Ledges during World War One. The sailors made it to a boat and landed on Gannet, where the keeper took them in.

More than two decades later, marine agent H. F. Morrissey contacted Kay's father on Gannet Rock. "If you see any suspicious-looking craft please notify me immediately," he wrote. "If it is a submarine call it 'Load of Hay.' Be careful not to mention the word submarine over the telephone."

Soldiers installing the six-inch guns at Chebucto Head, 1942–43.

THE ARMY AND CHEBUCTO HEAD

For lightkeepers and their families living near Halifax during World War Two, there were daily reminders that the world was in turmoil. Founded as a garrison town in 1749, conflict had been the city's bread and butter for two centuries. An extensive system of fortifications had evolved over the years, and by 1939, walled forts, guns, searchlights and submarine nets protected the strategic North Atlantic naval port.

By 1940, Britain was dependent on Halifax as a jumping-off point for thousands of Allied troops heading overseas. Hitler had already secured most of the western European ports, and as Britain held fast against German attacks, enemy forces made their way to our waters.

During a visit in 1943, Sir Winston Churchill let Haligonians know their war efforts were crucial to the world, when he told the mayor, "Now, sir, we know your city is something more than a shed on a wharf."

Keepers at Chebucto Head and McNabs Island witnessed it all—the parade of convoys heading to England, the flame and smoke of torpedoed ships, the fighter planes of Eastern Air Command. For young Don Gallagher, there was even more. Living at Chebucto Head, he was in the thick of all things military.

Around 1940 the government decided it wanted to erect a gun battery atop the thirty-metre granite cliff overlooking the harbour approaches. They demolished the lighthouse and keepers' houses and levelled the top of the cliff in preparation for building. From their new home, a wooden lighthouse on the edge of the cliff to the north, Don watched as a bustling fortification grew.

When I spoke with him, Don was happy to share this story of the "brilliant minds" who decided where the powerful searchlights at the bottom of the cliff would go. "You wouldn't believe the system they used to put these things down there," he said. "They had this elaborate ramp—it took months to build this thing and they took these search lights down on trailers. I was only a young kid but obviously there was a better way of doing it!" Why not deliver everything by water—the same way lighthouse supplies had been delivered for decades?

After much effort workers slid the searchlights down the ramp and installed them in their concrete buildings. But something wasn't quite right, as Don and his brothers noticed.

"We knew what was going to happen," Don recalled. "Military secrets! We knew they were going to turn on the lights and they wouldn't shine on the water! They forgot that the rocks out in front were *higher* than the beam of the light!"

No matter. A little more dynamite and the top of the offending rocks came off, allowing the searchlight beams to shine out to sea. Great.

No obstructions between the blazing lights and enemy vessels skulking along the coast. But the blasting had now exposed the nearby foghorn building to another enemy: the sea.

"I was down in the fog alarm building helping Dad one night," Don told me. "We were in the back room—I used to call it the quiet room 'cause with those diesels, you couldn't stand it out in the main room—and Dad was lying on an old hard bunk, reading. We had the door closed to the outside room when we heard the engine start to slow down.

"The two of us went out and were met by about a foot and a half of salt water. The sea had come right through and smashed the front doors in! The water was so deep that the big, giant flywheel on the engine was slowing the engine down.

"More cursing out of Dad—the army, the war, Hitler—a few things he wasn't too crazy about!" Don said, shaking his head and laughing. "Then he had to tear the engines all to pieces because they were full of saltwater.

To this day, if you look closely you can see lighter patches on the rocks where the dynamite did its work. Don still loves pointing that out when he shares his stories of government engineers.

Blasting work overhead also placed Edward Gallagher at risk as he stood his watch in the engine room. Don told me, "Dad was in the back room, with the fog alarm goin', and they'd set off five hundred cases of dynamite a hundred feet above his head."

During one blasting session, a rock "half the size of a dining room table" smashed through the building's slate roof, landing on the concrete floor between the foghorn engines and bringing a shocked Edward Gallagher running to see what the hell was going on.

"One of the workers looked down over the cliff and, seeing the damaged roof, started down to see if anyone was hurt," Don remembered. "The guy didn't get ten feet when he met my dad coming up the steps."

The worker started to say something, but an irate Edward Gallagher immediately cut him short, noting that if he didn't keep his mouth shut, he'd "stuff him in the hole to keep the rain out."

When the blasting was over and the construction complete, Chebucto Head was changed forever. Above the searchlights, where the lighthouse had been, three six-inch gun batteries had a commanding view of the harbour. Deep beneath the cape, men in the plotting room analyzed target bearings taken from observation posts spread south along the shore towards Ketch Harbour. At the bottom of the hill in Duncan's Cove, various mess halls and living quarters for military personnel vied for space with barracks for enlisted men, and a parade square, recreation hall, hospital, chapel, barber shop, and pump house.

Don told me there were usually between three hundred and seven hundred men from various units stationed at Chebucto Head. The radar tower (now converted to a luxury seaside mansion) near Duncan's Cove was run by the navy, and according to Don, the local army guys were always getting into scraps with the navy men. "Get your coke bottles" was the usual prelude to a fight, Don explained, and the hospital was always busy on Sundays, as doctors and nurses repaired the damage from weekend skirmishes.

The navy also kept some of its equipment in the attic of the Gallagher home, just below the lantern. Catherine Gallagher was not impressed that her house was open to strangers twenty-four hours a day as they came and went from their nook in the attic. But she was touched by one young man's story.

Many of the men who worked at the radar site were posted there to recover from war-related trauma. One fellow was just eighteen. He'd been on the *Athabaskan* in the English Channel when it was torpedoed, right beneath his feet, and 129 of his mates went down with their ship. The Germans took 83 survivors as prisoners and another Canadian destroyer picked up 44 sailors.

"He was burned a bit, but the worst was his nerves," Don said. "He was very jumpy. My Mum would say, 'What a nice young man. I wonder if he will ever be okay.'

"All my father would say was, 'Damn Hitler and his subs!'"

The Gallaghers also saw action from the vantage point of their lighthouse home—the glare of burning vessels, and Canadian ships patrolling for U-boats. Don says that sometimes the navy didn't even need to be engaged in battle to find itself in trouble.

"One of our famous navy ships was going around in circles in the fog, looking for a U-boat. For some reason he decided Ketch Harbour was Halifax Harbour and promptly deposited his boat on Splitnose Point. He must have been flying because he was well clear of the water. You could see right under the keel!"

One sailor was hurt by the impact—Don said a man cut his hand badly while opening a can of something or other at the time of the crunch. The navy towed the vessel off the next day. Although "the bow was smucked up a bit," it was "nothing a can of paint wouldn't cure," Don remembered with a laugh.

On blackout nights the atmosphere was eerie. One night a U-boat presence forced a convoy of dozens of ships to literally *back* into the harbour after setting out to sea. With the lighthouse beam doused, everything was inky black. "You could hear the ships," Don said, "but you couldn't see them—maybe just a silhouette once in a while."

THE WAR WASN'T
THAT FAR AWAY AT ALL

Farther up the harbour at McNabs Island, wartime life for the Cleveland family was very busy. Their lighthouse sat north of the Maugher's Beach light, just down the road from one of the island's four forts and gun batteries. McNabs had been a strategic part of the Halifax defence system for decades, and the war brought abandoned forts out of dormancy. A submarine net spanned from the end of Maugher's Beach to York Redoubt, guarded by two gate ships.

The war "brought a lot of army people there training," Joan (Cleveland) McGregor told me. "We had young soldiers, we had the officers where they were friends of the family. They took over the forts and made them operable."

The McNabs Island lighthouse was a natural gathering place for soldiers looking for a break from the tedium of duty. The Cleveland family's hospitality and fresh milk (from their own cows), to say nothing of their four lovely daughters, were a sure draw.

The McNabs Island lighthouse was a natural gathering place for World War Two soldiers stationed nearby.

More than sixty years later, a delightful and youthful-looking Joan smiled as she remembered the war years. "To me it was exciting and I used to feel a little guilty sometimes because why was this so much fun? There was never anyone in our immediate family that was overseas and killed, so maybe the war was a little remote for us—our impressions of the war were what we heard on the radio for reports."

But sometimes the excitement turned to danger.

"We came home from playing with the neighbour kids one evening," Joan told me "and there was a terrible smell of oil fumes in the air. Our house was in darkness. My parents were in their bedroom and they called to us as we came in the yard. 'Don't light a match!' they said. "Then they told us that they had seen a ship afire off Chebucto Head. It was an oil tanker that had been torpedoed out there, in full sight.

"Within days they had towed the stern end of the ship around Maughers Beach and into the garrison pier. The front half of the ship burned for three weeks out there."

The Clevelands soon made friends with the Norwegian crew of the vessel. "They used to take us out aboard this stern end of the ship and they would put on sumptuous meals," Joan recalled. "Eventually they towed it into the shipyards in Halifax and they put a bulkhead in it so it was seaworthy. They towed that out the harbour and all the way to New York, where they were going to put a front end onto the ship.

"When they went out it was planned that we were to be up on the lighthouse, with a flag and we would salute them as they went out. They saluted us as they went out. It was very touching, really."

On another occasion, a close call for a sailor boyfriend of Marjorie, the oldest sister, made all those radio reports seem less remote. "She knew he was going," Joan said, "and she watched that ship go out. Well, that ship was sunk right off the harbour. But the boyfriend wasn't killed in it, luckily."

Joan paused, remembering that day.

"No, the war wasn't that far away at all."

IT WAS BETTER THAN LIVING IN THE CITY!

Joan Cleveland might have felt guilty about the good times that war brought to McNabs Island, but she wasn't alone. Back at Chebucto Head, every day was a new adventure for Don Gallagher. As long as he'd finished his homework after school, he was free to run down the hill to take in a movie at the army recreation hall. "Every night of the week if you wanted to go to a movie you could go to a different one," he said. "It was better than living in the city!"

Apart from the movies, the army hosted card games, bingos, dances, and stage shows, and they had a hockey team and a baseball

One of the six-inch guns at Chebucto Head.

team. "There was never a dull moment!" Don said. "And just to liven things up they would fire those big guns!" Amidst the granite-shaking blasts, Don's mother would rush to remove a few dishes off the shelves in the lighthouse kitchen to prevent any collateral damage to the china.

Then there was the food. Don told me about a cook who tried to observe the eating habits of the men of various religious backgrounds— for example, the Catholic tradition of eating fish instead of meat on Fridays. The cook made a deal with Don's father Edward to supply him with fresh haddock for fish day. So every Thursday afternoon Don and his brothers rowed out to the "Cape Cove" to where there was a "muddy bottom, just great for haddock."

After bringing their catch ashore and hauling it to the top of the cliff they'd be met by an army jeep that would carry it down to the mess hall. "I guess the guys from Upper Canada and out west loved it," Don said. He adds that his family didn't consider the fish fresh if "it wasn't wiggling when you put it in the pan."

In return for wiggling fish, the army supplied the Gallaghers with groceries. The first delivery was a bit of a shocker. One morning a three-quarter-ton truck arrived at the lighthouse with a driver and two men. They asked the lightkeeper where he wanted the groceries put and Edward, thinking it would be a box or two, answered, "Just put them in the porch, please."

The men started to unload the truck into what appeared to be an increasingly small porch. First there was a side of beef. Then, forty-eight loaves of bread, gallons of milk, and impossibly large quantities of cheese, butter, and flour. "Holy @#&*!" Edward exclaimed. "I'm not trying to open a grocery chain!"

As Don remembered, he and his brothers had provided the army with no more than ten dollars' worth of fish, for which they had received about five hundred dollars' worth of groceries. "It took a couple of months of fish deliveries to get the army down to sizeable amounts of food," he said, laughing. In the end, the Gallaghers were able to order what and how much they wanted. In a time of strict rationing for most folks, it was a real help to the family.

THE END OF WAR

By 1944, the end was in sight. Germany began the surrender and retreat from their conquests in the Crimea and Anzio, while Soviet troops liberated the first concentration camp at Majdanek. The D-Day landings in Normandy on June 6, 1944, showed further cracks in the German armour.

Back on this side of the Atlantic, the news gripped lighthouse families. Kay Ingersoll still remembers the day like it was yesterday. A supply boat was tied in the gulch below the big white-and-black-striped lighthouse on Gannet Rock. A gentle sea stirred the rockweed in the clear Bay of Fundy waters. "My mother came out on the deck, and called down to us and said, 'The Allies have landed in France!'" she told me. "I can see her standing there. That was a big deal. I always think of it every time they mention D-Day! I think of my mother standing out there on Gannet Rock."

Life started to return to normal for lightkeepers and their families. By the middle of November 1944, the government disbanded the Aircraft Detection Corps "in view of the more favourable progress of the war…" Across the Atlantic, Hitler's hold on Europe was weakening. Faced with an unrelenting Allied advance and erosion of his own control, Hitler committed suicide at the end of April 1945. One week later German forces surrendered unconditionally to Allied forces.

The time-consuming A, B, C instructions that had forced so many keepers to live their lives in four-hour chunks ended on June 18, 1945, a little more than a month after V-E Day.

But it wasn't over yet.

Halfway around the world the Americans were getting ready to drop an atomic bomb on Hiroshima. On August 5, 1945, the *Enola Gay*, a B-29 bomber dropped "Little Boy," the name given to the 4,100 kilogram uranium bomb that would flatten much of the city. By the end of the year an estimated 140,000 people had died, either from the direct impact or from exposure to radiation. A further 60,000 died later, in the contaminated wreckage of their city.

In her last book, *B was for Butter and Enemy Craft*, Evelyn Richardson wrote words that have an eerie foreboding to this day:

"A few days later peace was proclaimed. A peace trailing the Cold War and the Balance of Nuclear Terror. Not yet have we heard 'C for Charlie. The danger is past.'"

10

The End of the Lightkeeper

A COUPLE OF TIMES A YEAR, I LIKE to drive along Nova Scotia's South Shore, stopping in at various lights along the way. After all, this is the Lighthouse Route, as designated by the provincial government's tourism department. Generally, I stay away from Peggy's Cove. Although it has a nice lighthouse, the place has lost its appeal for me—too many tour buses and too many tourists scrambling over the granite at the edge of the sea.

So, I cruise along Highway 3, past Lunenburg, to Port Medway. There's a beautiful little wooden harbour light there, lovingly restored by the community. It sits on the site of the village's former fish plant, now a landscaped park complete with a bandstand and a panoramic view of the harbour.

Abandoned buildings at Cape Roseway

Then it's off to Liverpool, home to diarist Simeon Perkins, novelist Thomas Raddall, and the hunchbacked Fort Point lighthouse, perched at the edge of Liverpool Bay. Like at Port Medway, local residents helped rescue the little light after the Coast Guard had turned it off and let the tower sit, empty and dark, for a decade. Now restored, with a gift shop and museum inside—and public toilets attached—it beckons loads of visitors who come to snap photos and buy souvenirs.

But I want a real lighthouse. One with a working light and a foghorn and a big sea surging against the rocks. So I turn back into town and left onto the road leading past Moose Harbour, to Western Head. If it's foggy and I stop at the top of Lighthouse Road, I can hear the horn—one long, six-second monotone blast every minute, echoing out to sea.

I turn down Lighthouse Road. There's the white tower, red lantern, light flashing. The horn blasts again. It's damp and windy. Now this is a *real* lighthouse.

But where is the keeper's house? Where are the garage, the foghorn building, the picket fences, the painted stones lining the driveway, the Canadian flag straining against a snapping halyard? Where is the lightkeeper?

He's been gone for the better part of two decades. Where his house stood, there's a pile of fill enclosed within a chain-link fence, and four funny-looking posts set on each corner. This is now part of the Differential GPS (DGPS) network, the navigation system which has made lights and horns largely obsolete.

Another blast of the horn. I think back to the early 1980s, when I first drove down the road to Western Head with my father. We were on our way home from an aborted trip to Seal Island, and I had persuaded my dad to indulge me in at least one lighthouse on the way back.

We met the keeper, Lemuel Moreau, and he took us into the big, rambling foghorn building. Lemuel had the whole place painted up—from the white ceilings, to the high-gloss, battleship-grey floors. He explained how he reported the weather, and logged the Coast Guard helicopter's trips to his lighthouse for fuel.

Everything was immaculate and in its proper place—even the wrenches had hooks and little outlines drawn on the wall so you'd know where they belonged. On that day, Lemuel symbolized for me the pride and attention to detail that marked his profession, even after most of his duties had been taken away by automated equipment.

By 1988, even though Lemuel was still on the station, the whole kit and kaboodle was monitored from afar. If he wanted to get into the tower, he had to call the keepers at Cape Forchu to disable the intrusion alarm. He didn't even have to climb the lighthouse tower to clean the lantern windows or squeeze a little oil into the light's rotating mechanism.

Lemuel told me at the time, "I don't know what it's working like now. I haven't been up there…" and he trailed off, trying to remember just when it was he had last been up in his lighthouse.

Today, the light is still there, lens turning 24-7. All that's left of the old foghorn building is a concrete pad, with no trace of the high-gloss floor paint.

Lightkeeper Lemuel Moreau at Western Head in 1988.

The fog detector, the back-up engines, the radios—everything is now stuffed into the lighthouse, which stands as the only reminder that this is indeed a lightstation.

No Lemuel and Geraldine Moreau, welcoming a visitor in for a cup of coffee on a cold day. No more stories of storms, visitors, and Coast Guard characters.

On the way out, I stop just past the DGPS towers. There, among the stunted spruce and alders, is a rotten section of picket fence. It is the only other reminder here that Western Head was once a busy, proud, and painted-up lightstation.

The story of Western Head is the story of almost every lighthouse in the Maritimes. True, some have been saved by local groups, and stand

proud as reminders of our lightkeeping past. But most just sit, mould-
ering into the ground. Many others have been burned, bulldozed, and
beaten into memory.

The death of lightkeeping took place over a relatively short period
of time in the grand scheme of lighthouse history. Until the early 1960s,
many Canadian lighthouses operated as they had since the French built
the stone light at Louisbourg in 1733. Keepers lit their kerosene-pow-
ered lights each evening and cranked up the weights that helped rotate
big lenses floating on baths of mercury.

Well into the 1950s, they kept an ear cocked for the sound of a
vessel's horn, in order to hurl a reply into the fog with a hand-pow-
ered foghorn. Most island lights didn't have electricity until the 1950s;
lightkeepers heated their homes with wood and coal. And keepers did
everything, from lighting lamps, to tearing engines apart, to planting
cabbages in the spring.

But by the early 1960s there were ominous changes in the wind.
Electricity and mod-cons for isolated lightkeepers soon became the
norm, but they marked the beginning of the end of lightkeeping in
Nova Scotia.

It was a change more or less in line with what was happening
around the world. In his account of lightkeeping in England during the
late 1950s, Arthur Lane notes with some concern that the old ways were
coming to an end.

> There were too many engines, too much noise, too much
> technology providing points of contact with the outside world.
> I like machinery; it is much easier to understand than people;
> but the silence of the night watches was no longer broken only
> by the hiss of the Hood Burner, the gentle groaning of the lens
> clock, and the summer slop or winter roar of the sea. There
> was the intrusive Radio-Telephone and the twelve minute cycle
> of the radio beacon. Most threatening of all…there was televi-
> sion and the first-heard commercial jingle about someone's ice
> cream, a memory trace to be expunged only by death.

In 1968 the federal government decided that lightkeepers were costing the Canadian taxpayer too much money, and thus began the process to automate and de-staff Canadian lighthouses. By 1972, the Canadian Coast Guard had installed new equipment at most Canadian lightstations—and in the process, removed almost three centuries' worth of duties and dedication.

Destaffing day at Cross Island, July 10, 1989. A Coast Guard helicopter prepares to sling George Locke's belongings to the mainland.

Whether we need lightkeepers today is, for the most part, a moot point. Around fifty automated stations still have on-site staff in British Columbia and Newfoundland. On the west coast, lightkeepers still provide points of comfort and assistance for people working and travelling along a remote, sparsely populated coast.

In Newfoundland, a high unemployment rate combined with political pressure has left a few stations open, with lightkeepers acting as groundskeepers and tour guides. How useful is this for the mariner, when most of the remote stations in Newfoundland have been closed in favour of retaining keepers on mainland sites? Does it matter?

One fact is certain: The end of lightkeeping was, for the most part, a morale-sucking, three-decade-long affair that soured a lot of people who had devoted their entire lives to lighthouses.

The sheer numbers tell part of the story. In the mid-1950s, there were more than 350 lights in Nova Scotia, including 170 conventional wooden or concrete towers. More than 100 of these had regular or attendant keepers. By 1972, only 62 lights still had on-site keepers. By then, their lights were turning twenty-four hours a day, and the Coast Guard had replaced the old diaphones and hand horns with automated electronic emitters. Keepers were left with menial chores and a hands-off policy towards any of the new equipment.

During the 1980s, forty-five Nova Scotia lights lost their keepers. It was a busy time for Coast Guard crews, as they crated up family furniture and slung helicopter-loads of belongings off headlands and islands. Lighthouse legend has it that in their hurry to nail plywood on the doors and windows of the buildings at one station, an overzealous Coast Guard work crew inadvertently boarded a lightkeeper into his own house!

By 1993, with the unceremonious closure of Yarmouth's Cape Forchu lighthouse, there was nothing left to board up (and no one to board *in*). Today, Nova Scotia's physical lighthouse heritage has all but disappeared. What remains of our lightkeeping tradition is locked away in the heads of the folks who lived the life.

Here's what they remember about the way it ended.

LIGHTKEEPERS TOOK
PRIDE IN THEIR STATION

George Locke began lightkeeping in 1975, when the move to automate Nova Scotia's lights was well underway. Still, when George and
his family moved to barren Country Island in Guysborough County,
vestiges of the old pride remained. George and head keeper Vernon
Zwicker kept the station buildings sparkling white and red. At two
o'clock in the morning—the beginning of his daily watch—George
faithfully made the trek along a long boardwalk to the automated
engine room to make sure the generators were running smoothly.

George and Vernon were ever-watchful over the lobster fishermen
out of nearby Drum Head, New Harbour and Seal Harbour, hauling
traps off the island.

George Locke: "They took
the pride out of the job."

Even though the time-consuming work of maintaining kerosene lights and diesel-powered foghorns was a thing of the past, there was still enough work to keep the men busy, and to give them a sense of purpose in the job.

"Lightkeepers took pride in their stations," George told me. "We had a lot of visitors and when somebody come on my station I didn't want them to go away and say the station was dirty or ill-run. Ninety per cent of the lightkeepers were the same way. Years ago, the Coast Guard would come around inspect the station. You'd get a letter back sayin' how well the station was kept or whether it wasn't kept!"

Fourteen years later, when he left Lunenburg's Cross Island, George had a different view of lightkeeping. That pride, he said, "all died in the eighties. The ones that run it didn't care. The same as today. Nobody in the Coast Guard cares anymore. The only thing they care about is keepin' jobs in the office. They took the pride out of the job." He added: "We had one manager who was gettin' paid for job hours that he got clear of. He was gettin' a bonus [when] he closed down more lights. He even closed lights down ahead of when they were scheduled to close, because he was gettin' a bonus to do it! So when you find that out and when you start askin' for stuff to keep your station clean and can't get it, the pride's gotta go out of your job. And that's what killed lightkeepin'."

It's been seventeen years since George left Cross Island, and more than a decade since Nova Scotia's last lightkeepers left their posts. But George's bitterness over the way the feds treated lightkeepers and lighthouses still rises to the surface easily.

"We have a government that just don't care anymore," he said to me, disgustedly. "You go along the coast today, it's a goddamn disgrace. If you can go on one station that has been unmanned and say that it's a well-kept station or looks anything like a government institution you better name it now. Because we haven't got them on the coast."

It's always easy to complain about the government. It is a Canadian pastime to scorn the bureaucracy that we see at times as sluggish, inefficient, costly and too-far removed from everyday life. But George's complaints aren't idle Ottawa-bashing banter. For him, it's just hard to look at what is left of the fourteen years he put into lightkeeping.

The ransacked interior of the assistant keeper's house on Cross Island.

"Cross Island is a pigsty. The walls are beat down, the cisterns are plugged up, people have crapped in the rooms in the house, the carpets are all rotten, windows are all out of it, and they still haven't got money to tear down a building.

"Far as I'm concerned what's happened along this coast is a disgrace, and it's a disgrace to every Canadian that ever *ever* thought that a lighthouse was nice. 'Cause there's no such thing as a nice lighthouse on the coast."

In the same breath, George allows that even when he started the job, keepers were obsolete.

"I loved the job, but I'll admit we don't need keepers. With the equipment today, we don't need 'em. Some of these lobster boats, they got more equipment into 'em than what the big boats have. There's still a few that go by compass, but the equipment's there. The government subsidies are there to get it, there's good money in lobster and inshore fishin'. There's no need of a man goin' without. If he wants a radar, go buy it. It's tax deductible! Why not spend your tax deductible instead of givin' it to the government! You got GPS and that new equipment. It'd be nice to have people watchin' the coast, but I'd be the first one to admit today that you don't need a lightkeeper."

Ingram Wolfe holds another view, despite the widespread use of electronic aids to navigation. Ingram did his share of search and rescue work while stationed on Mosher's Island (as did George Locke at Cross Island), at the entrance to the LaHave River on Nova Scotia's South Shore. In fact Ingram and his wife, Lynne, stayed on at Mosher's Island even after the station was officially automated. They finally left in 1991.

When I spoke to him recently, in his kitchen in Mount Pleasant, Lunenburg County, high above the Atlantic, he pretty well repeated what he'd said when CBC Television's *Land and Sea* interviewed him on Moshers Island almost twenty years ago.

"Well, I still think it's important to have lightkeepers. Today if you went to that station there'd be nobody there and there'd be nothing you could do if someone was in trouble. I've helped several people. There was a yacht upset one time in the harbour and there was four people aboard of that. I had to go off and rescue them outta the water. They probably would have been drowned if it wouldn't have been for me at the station.

"There was other times when boats got broke down and people got wound up in nets and they were drifting ashore or on the rocks. I don't know what would have happened—their boats would have broken up or maybe they would have drowned trying to get ashore.

"I still think that lightstations should have been left open," he added, "and there should have been at least one lightkeeper and his family for to keep those stations operating."

LEAVE IT UNTIL I'M GONE

Apart from the changing role of the lightkeeper and the lighthouse in the lives of mariners in the 1960s and '70s, life on the lights had also changed. Keepers had less to do and more time to do it. Sid Smith saw the whole progression at Cape Sable, from the pre-electricity days of the 1930s, to the "heyday" of lightkeeping in the 1960s, where three keepers kept watch over an assortment of engines, compressors and gauges, to the 1970s, when automated, solid-state electronics made their appearance.

"I stayed until '79," he told me, "but by then automation had gotten to the point where it spoiled all the nice things about lightkeeping.

We lost the old diaphone and many other things and it got to be just a mow-the-lawn-and-paint type of existence. 'Course the more they auto-mated, the bigger my garden got and the more cattle I had!"

Sid was often frustrated by the government's efforts to modernize equipment at Cape Sable.

"Well, they wanted to get rid of the old Fresnel lens because that was floating in a mercury bath. That was at the time when the big mercury scare was on. As a country we seem to go through these scares! First it's mercury, then it's something else. I don't suppose there was very many places that had more mercury on them than lightstations at that time. They were always gonna come and take it out and I said, 'Leave it until I'm gone!'

"Then they'd be back in the helicopter with the superintendent of lights or the engineer. 'Gotta get rid of that mechanism!' they said."

During one visit Sid asked the engineer what the Coast Guard planned to do with the mercury. Well, they were going to get rid of it. Sid replied, 'No, you don't just up and dispose of mercury. It's one of those things that you push down here but it's gonna come up some-where else.'

"'Oh, we'll do the proper thing,' the engineer said. So I said, 'Okay, can you do any better than this? Have the mercury on an isolated island, in a concrete tower in a cast iron vat, with two watchmen twenty-four hours a day watching over it! It's serving a purpose and when I'm gone you can do whatever you want, but as long as I'm here I want that mechanism there on top of the light.'" Sid smiled. "I don't know if I got away with it or they didn't get around to it while I was there, but I'm glad it stayed there as long as I was."

A few miles to the east, out on the barren Salvages, Jim Guptill was uneasy about the changes that were turning him and his partner into seaside janitors.

"We lost our generators in favour of the undersea cable," Jim told me. "Most of the things that we were doing for pastime—looking after the generators, the exterior painting—were gone. In the 1980s, safety became an issue, and they told us it was too rugged for two men to paint the place. The Coast Guard said they'd bring a ship down, and bring the crew ashore to do the work, and 'you can help.'"

At the time it may have seemed like a reprieve from an endless, time-consuming chore. But all it did for Jim was underscore the reality that things were on the downward swing at Salvages.

"What's the point of painting?" The Salvages lightstation shows its age shortly before automation in 1987.

"I put in ten years on the Salvages. That changed my view of things somewhat. It got to be an uncertainty. Initially, you were doing it because this is a good lifestyle, number one. It gives you time to do things—study, read, write. It was pretty good pay. But by the early- to mid-eighties, you knew that it was coming to an end and you'd lost that security."

That loss of security had a direct effect on morale at the station. As Jim said to me, "You lost interest. What's the point of painting when they could come in a month and announce that you're gone?"

That's exactly what happened in late 1986. It was a bleak winter day with "a stiffening nor'easter, with threatening snow and dark lowering skies. Quite dreary," he added.

One of the Coast Guard's Dartmouth District helicopters, a big shiny red Bell 212, dropped out of the sky to perch on the Salvages' helipad. As Jim recalls, things happened pretty fast.

"The helicopter picked us up off the station and flew us to Bridgewater, to a hotel. They left the lighthouse empty, unguarded and took both of us. We stopped at Gull Rock and took both of the keepers there. Then we stopped at Cape Roseway and took them.

"In Bridgewater they announced, 'You're out of work,' and that they were shutting us down within the year and then they took us back and let us out and flew away.

"I don't mind telling you I was really pissed off about that. I thought the Coast Guard was unacceptably crass. Christmas is looming ahead of me. I'm going to be away from home and I won't see my family again for three more weeks and I got no work!"

Jim was pretty unhappy about it all, but time lessened his anger. "It was from a lack of understanding on the Coast Guard's part," he told me, "not of meanness. Don't get me wrong. They didn't recognize that when we were set back on Salvages and the helicopter flew away, we had *nothing!* No job, no future, no security."

Fortunately, things worked out for Jim. He stayed on with the federal government, working at the Coast Guard's Regional Operations Centre in Dartmouth. He even moved back to a lighthouse at Chebucto Head, where, after pulling his shift in town, he was the *in situ* caretaker.

But back in December 1986, the future didn't look too bright.

To be fair, the Coast Guard did not pull the rug out from under their lightkeepers. Many stayed on station until their retirements. Others were trained and reassigned to Coast Guard ships, Coast Guard Radio, or went to work at the regional base in Dartmouth. Unlike the Scottish Lighthouse service, where redundant keepers in their forties and fifties had to scrabble to find new jobs—a friend of mine became a taxi driver—the Canadian Coast Guard didn't boot its keepers out to pasture. But the slow stagnation in the job, the uncertainty, and the declining morale, took their toll.

It turned us sick to go back there

It has been twenty years since the bulk of lighthouses in the Maritimes lost their keepers. For some, the bitter feelings have dulled, but they haven't disappeared. For others, there's no bitterness—just a sadness and a sense of loss.

Geraldine (Boutilier) Stevens' time on Croucher's Island, St. Margaret's Bay, in the 1920s and '30s still brings back strong memories for the eighty-four-year-old woman. Croucher's was an island paradise for children. Geraldine's parents, Wentworth and Maggie Boutilier, made the place a real home, with flower and vegetable gardens, an apple orchard, and a cosy nook with swings and hammocks, amidst the spruce trees.

Geraldine Boutilier (front right) poses with her family on Crouchers Island in 1928.

It was a pretty good life. The family was close. Wentworth taught his children to respect the weather and the water. Maggie was an expert wood splitter, and taught her kids the art. Croucher's was a good place to learn how to survive without many creature comforts.

I interviewed Geraldine in 2002. Sixty years after leaving the island, her feelings about Croucher's still ran strong. She told me how she had returned to the island years later with her brother Bert.

"It was the worst mistake we ever made," she said. "Where was Croucher's Island? What happened to it? All the land that Dad had in apple trees was nothin' but a heartbreaker to see. And Mum's garden and the nook—nothing left."

But there was one small reminder of the Boutilier family's life on Croucher's Island—a single white rose in bloom. For Geraldine it made the return to the island all that much more difficult to bear.

"It was Dad's rose bush. Sir Thomas Lipton was the name of it." She shook her head. "Oh! It turned us sick to go back there!"

Kelly (Fairservice) Brown left Sambro Island in 1988 when the Coast Guard de-staffed the station that had been her home for twenty-four years.

Her mother and father were both keepers there, and Kelly herself worked as a relief keeper when her folks went on vacation. Looking at photos of her old home, windows smashed out, shingles ripped off by the wind, and the interior gutted by vandals, she told me, "It makes my heart ache. Dad was very meticulous.

Run-down Sambro Island.

The grass was cut every seven days. His tools, you could eat off. The lawnmower, after you'd finished mowing the lawn, was cleaned and wiped down. Everything was so beautiful and white and neat and tidy.

"To see it in the shape that it is now, it's just a shame. It's too bad the government didn't appreciate what they had and looked after the place, because Sambro Island is an historic site and we should be a little bit more appreciative of our historic sites.

"On the other hand, you could dwell on it and be sad, but I would like to take my kids out there because it's still a beautiful place. Sure the dwellings are run down but you can stand on any point of that island and look and it's just beautiful from whatever direction.

"That's the way I *have* to look at it."

Sid Smith goes back to Cape Sable once or twice a year. The place has changed radically from his days as a keeper—all that's left today is the lighthouse, and some outlines and depressions in the ground where the houses, barn, sheds and fog alarm once stood.

Sid Smith returns to Cape Sable every year. Only the lighthouse remains at his former home.

Sid is pretty pragmatic about the changes that have left the cape a barren, grass-covered piece of real estate marked only by the massive, deteriorating concrete light tower. On a recent visit, he went back to see what was left of his family home.

"Usually I don't go down around where the station was at all," he said to me, "but I cut right across there and I got figuring out, 'Okay, now that rock there that would tell me where the barn was. If the barn was there, the well would have been out here and this is where the temperature screen was. And here's where the corner of the house would be.'

"I fooled around there for fifteen to twenty minutes and I think I pretty well laid out right where the buildings used to be, even though they've been long gone.

"Yeah, it's kind of sad to me to see that they don't keep up their lighthouses after the lightkeepers were taken off. I was up in that tower

Sid and Betty June Smith at Cape Sable in the 1950s.

this past summer. I suppose somebody must go up there to the top of it once in a while, but all the paint is just hanging. It's really sad to go in and I'd wished I hadn't gone up there because if somebody had said it was in a real mess, well, I wouldn't have envisioned anything *that* bad.

"When they got rid of the Pony Express, they didn't kill all the horses," he added, "so when lighthouses aren't necessary anymore, it doesn't mean that you should just let 'em fall down."

But in the same breath Sid said he was also glad the buildings are gone without a trace. Better to have the station turned back to nature than crowded with decaying structures—rotting reminders of the past.

Bernice Goodick agrees. When she visits what's left of the Cape Roseway lightstation, she's stricken with a sadness made all the stronger by memories of the lively and well-kept place it was in the 1950s. "It's unkempt, falling down," she told me. "The Coast Guard should just go in there and flatten *everything* and let the sheep take over."

To me it's a tragedy that the once fine stations at Cape Sable and Cape Roseway have been reduced to a crumbling towers and, in the case of Cape Roseway, a collection of rotting buildings, but Sid gets me thinking when he tells me that no matter what *his* old home looks like now, *nothing* can take away the memories of the wonderful life he and his family shared there.

I THINK I'M THE
MOST FORTUNATE OF MEN

For some keepers, everything worked out in the end. Despite the sadness at the loss of their way of life, many appreciate the experience they had as lightkeepers. Jim Guptill put in twenty-seven years on the lights, and as I interviewed him in a conference room in a busy downtown Halifax office building, he summed up his experiences as a lightkeeper.

"I think I'm the most fortunate of men. I went through a period in history that had never happened before. They say history repeats itself. That part of it has never done. Nor will it, I don't think. So I was privileged to be a part of that transition between an old century and the new one.

"When we went on Country Island in September of 1960, there was nothing modern there. We had to carry our water from the well. We had to go to the old outhouse. The light ran on kerosene. Everything was the same as it had been for three hundred years. Nothing had changed.

"Then in the mid sixties, they built a new modern station on Country Island. There was generators and suddenly we had televisions in our home and hot and cold running water. We're still isolated, but the isolation, the bite has been taken off it and it left us with mostly the good part of isolation, which is the control over your circumstances and surroundings.

"And then to go complete cycle to the place where there was no lightkeeping responsibilities at all…1960 to 1987 is a work-life for most people. It was a marvellous experience.

"I can't think of anything that I would have done to change it," Jim asserted. "If I was fifteen years old again right now and had the choice of knowing what I know now, I'd still do it."

Epilogue

WHEN I LOOK BACK AT MY INTERVIEWS WITH lightkeepers and their families, I am struck by the contrast between the vitality of their stories, and how little is left of the lights they called home.

Each time I came away from an interview I felt transported back in time, half expecting to be able to visit some of these lights and find them intact and full of life.

Unfortunately, a trip to many of Nova Scotia's lighthouses reveals weather-beaten towers and empty, ransacked houses. True, a handful have been restored and are now lovingly maintained by communities, so that visitors can get a sense at least of what it might have been like to live at a lighthouse. Nova Scotians living in coastal villages are intensely proud of their Maritime heritage and their hard labour saved beacons in places such as Cape Forchu, Port Bickerton, Hampton and Sandy Point. And for more than a decade, the Nova Scotia Lighthouse Preservation Society has fought to keep our lights in the public domain and lobbied on behalf of lighthouse communities.

The Port Medway lighthouse sat abandoned for more than a decade...

...until local residents decided to save it. The tower is now a focal point of the village waterfront.

But in many cases, our lights have slipped into the past. Although the government is more mindful of public interest in our lighthouse heritage than it once was—from the 1960s to the 1980s, Coast Guard crews often burned keeperless lightstation buildings to the ground without any public notice—there's not much left to save.

What's left is still at risk. In 2004, Nova Scotia lost two lighthouses to fire: Don Gallagher's old home at Chebucto Head and the century-old wooden lighthouse at Pictou Bar. Both fires were likely set by vandals. So, between government policy, disuse and vandalism, our lights have taken a real hit.

Even the Sambro Island lighthouse, the oldest operating lightstation in the Western Hemisphere, has been neglected by the Canadian government. Although they restored the exterior of the tower in 1998, the feds have ignored the keepers' houses and old gas house on an island that should be a national monument to lightkeeping.

Our keepers and their families are taking a hit too, as mortality chips away at a dwindling number of people who gave their lives to the protection of seafarers around our coasts. Already, seven of the people who told me their stories have died—Jean Barkhouse, Blair Cameron, Anne Flemming, Andy Hodder, Wick Lent, Adalene McSheffery and Waldo Haines. With them goes the collective experience of a singular and never-to-be-repeated way of life.

So I'm happy that I have been able to save some of that experience. It was a privilege to be allowed into that world and to share stories with friends and with complete strangers who have become friends as a result of this project.

I can still see Melda DeBaie—despite her willingness to tell me how much she hated growing up at Owl's Head light—with her eyes closed, saying "I can see every rock and every stone and every cliff. Oh, I can see it all! It's engraved in me mind forever."

I have to laugh as I remember Grace Cahill answering my question about how often she thought about the old days at the Hubbards light.

"Well how many days are there a year? Three hundred and sixty-five. That's the answer. Every day of my life. I was the only one out of the whole crowd that always got homesick. I was down there all during the war and Papa used to say, 'There comes Grace. Give any of the rest of them a hundred dollars, they wouldn't stay overnight! Give Grace five cents and she'll stay a year!'"

When I tried to get to the heart of just why Grace loved her lighthouse home, she shot back "There was nothin' there, when you come to think about it. I had a very crude home, as you know. You went up them friggin' old steps with a bannister on it."

Anne Richardson with her sister Betty June on Bon Portage Island

Then she added, laughing: "That's not really anything that I would like anybody to read about, because they might be jealous!"

But what best sums up the experience for me is the last few lines I transcribed from my interview with Anne Wickens.

"I was a very antisocial child. I hated to see company coming. I would get fond of some of the relatives, but I was always glad to see them go, just the same. To this day, I do not like people as people. I don't like crowds, I don't like lots of people talking, I don't like gatherings of any kind. I get up and speak in front of them and carry on as if this is normal procedure, but I just don't like them.

"What bothers me is: Where do people today go, to find a place without people, where there's just themselves and nature? I mean as a family, or as an individual. In a great many lives it can't be done. I have always prized the fact that I had that on Bon Portage. And frankly I miss it yet."

Acknowledgements

THIS PROJECT HAS BEEN A HUGE UNDERTAKING THAT would not have been possible without the help of dozens of former lightkeepers and their families. I will be forever grateful for their generous support and hospitality. Although I did not use every interview in this book, all of the material I collected is reflected in the stories within.

Thanks to lighthouse people Dorothy Kiley, Anne and Sara Flemming, Donald Wickerson Lent, Harry Lent, Ingram and Lynne Wolfe, Andrew and Lillian Hodder, Ivan and Mildred Kent, Dale Veinot, Kelly Brown, John and Marjorie Fairservice, Patti Young, Jean and Bobby Barkhouse, Ivan Langille, Joan McGregor, Faye Power, Adalene McSheffery, Russell Latimer, Percy Kehoe, Waldo Haines, Darla Fleet, Grace Cahill, Marie Stevens, Melda DeBaie, Kathleen Major, Alice Breau, Ina and Dorothy Yorke, Minnie Smith, Gordon Jewers, Stewart Gilkie, Blair Cameron, Valerie Opas, Heather Turner, Ronald Kenney, Alfred Hopkins, Ronald and Bea Spinney, Daniel Locke, Lemuel and Geraldine Moreau, Peter Coletti and the descendants of Mary-Ellen Reynolds.

Special thanks to Sid and Betty June Smith and Anne Wickens who were so consistently interested in and helpful with my own fascination with their lighthouse families. Their photos of Bon Portage and Cape Sable add immeasurable value to this book. Thanks also to Faye Lent, Geraldine Stevens, George Locke, Reg Smith, Jim Guptill, Kay Ingersoll, June Richardson and Muriel Smiley, who so generously shared their memories with me and allowed me to borrow and scan personal photographs showing a vanished way of life. I'd also like to acknowledge Don Gallagher's contributions to this book. Don is a neighbour, friend, and willing fount of information about the Chebucto Head lighthouse and World War Two fortifications there.

I must also acknowledge the Nova Scotia Lighthouse Preservation Society for their tireless work in lighthouse preservation. Interview material from Donald Gallagher, Anne and Sara Flemming, Andrew Hodder, Ivan and Mildred Kent, Dale Veinot, Kelly Brown, John and Marjorie Fairservice, Patti Young, Jean and Bobby Barkhouse, Joan McGregor, Faye Power, Darla

Fleet, Grace Cahill, Marie Stevens, Kathleen Major, Minnie Smith, Blair Cameron, Valerie Opas, and Heather Turner comes from the NSLPS "Lighthouse Life in Halifax Regional Municipality" oral history project.

Dan MacNeil of DFO/Canadian Coast Guard in Dartmouth was always willing and able to help with period photos and other lighthouse documents.

Thanks to Gerry Searles who made images of Three Top Island and of lightkeeper W. Munroe available to me.

Fiona Marshall's excellent master's thesis shed more light on Evelyn Richardson and her contributions to lightkeeping and the history of Shelburne County and I'd like to thank her for allowing me to quote from it. Miriam Walls of Parks Canada was helpful in locating hard-to-find images of wartime activities at Chebucto Head.

I am fortunate to have made the acquaintance of Arthur Lane, a former keeper at England's Eddystone Light. Arthur's observations about the social aspects of his lighthouse life made me think more carefully about the dynamic on Nova Scotia lighthouses.

I owe a great deal to my friend Rip Irwin, who for the past two decades has been a close lighthouse colleague and a kindred spirit in things nautical. Without him I would not have seen as many lighthouses and met as many keepers in Nova Scotia as I have.

Barry MacDonald has also been steadfast friend and partner in lighthouse endeavours over the past few years—thanks very much for your expertise and your interest in this project.

My good friends Dennis Stewart and Kathleen Allen put me up for a few nights and scanned borrowed photos for me while I collected material in southwest Nova Scotia—thanks for everything.

Thank you to Sandra McIntyre, Heather Bryan, and Penelope Jackson at Nimbus—your editorial expertise and your interest in this project made it a pleasure to prepare the book.

Eugene Meese also deserves thanks for helping me (mostly) kick the bad habit of passive writing.

I'd also like to thank my parents, Anne and Eric Mills, for taking me to the coast as a very young child and helping me cultivate my interest in all things lighthouse.

And finally, to my wife Seana, who not only put up with a constant "all-hit classic mix" of lighthouses while I wrote this book, but read it as it grew, offering useful and critical advice.

Thank you for your support.

Bibliograhpy

BOOKS:

Boutilier, Maggie B. *Life on Crouchers Island*. Tantallon: Glen Margaret Publishing, 2003.

Day, Frank Parker. *Rockbound*. Toronto: University of Toronto Press, 1989.

Graham, Donald. *Keepers of the Light: A History of British Columbia's Lighthouses and their Keepers*. Madeira Park: Harbour Publishing, 1985.

Graham, Donald. *Lights of the Inside Passage: A History of British Columbia's Lights and Their Keepers*. Madeira Park, BC: Harbour Publishing, 1986.

Gutsche, Andrea. *Alone in the Night: Lighthouses of Georgian Bay, Manitoulin Island and the North Channel*. Toronto: Lynx Images, 1996.

Flemming, Candace. *Women of the Lights*. Illinois: Albert Whitman and Company, 1996.

Floherty, John J. *Sentries of the Sea*. J. B. Lippincott, 1942.

Hamilton, Douglas. "Who Shot Estevan Light?" in *Raincoast Chronicles 18: Stories and History of the British Columbia Coast*, ed. Howard White. Madeira Park, BC: Harbour Publishing, 1998.

Irwin, E.H. Rip. *Lighthouses and Lights of Nova Scotia*. Halifax: Nimbus Publishing, 2003.

Lane, Arthur. *It Was Fun While It Lasted: Lighthouse Keeping in the 1950s*. Latheronwheel: Whittles Publishing, 1998.

Marshall, Fiona. *Nova Scotia's Lightkeeping Heritage: An Assessment of the Life and Work of Evelyn Richardson*. Halifax: Saint Mary's University, 2002.

Mills, Chris. *Vanishing Lights: A Lightkeeper's Fascination with a Disappearing Way of Life*. Hantsport: Lancelot Press, 1992.

Mitcham, Allison. *Offshore Islands of Nova Scotia and New Brunswick*. Hantsport: Lancelot Press, 1984.

Nova Scotia Lighthouse Preservation Society. *The Lightkeeper*. Issues from 1995-2006

Pullen, Hugh F., *The Sea Road to Halifax: Being an Account of the Lights and Buoys of Halifax Harbour*. Halifax: The Nova Scotia Museum, 1980.

Raddall, Thomas. *Halifax Warden of the North*. New York: Doubleday and Company, 1965.

Renton, Alan. *Lost Sounds: The Story of Coast Fog Signals*. Latheronwheel: Whittles Publishing, 2001.

Richardson, Evelyn. *We Keep A Light*. Toronto: Ryerson Press, 1945.

———. *B was for Butter and Enemy Craft*. Halifax: Petheric Press, 1976.

OTHER PUBLICATIONS AND SOURCES:

Bay News Vol 9, No. 11 December 1986.

Canadian Coast Guard and Department of Transport departmental correspondence, lightkeepers logs, and manuals from personal collection.

Chance Brothers. "The Diaphone: A Chance Product" (Undated company brochure).

Folster, David. "Shining for a Century and a Half" in Maclean's Magazine, January 4, 1982.

List of Lights, Buoys and Fog Signals, Atlantic Coast. Fisheries and Oceans, Ottawa 1977–2004.

Nova Scotia Lightouse Preservation Society. "Lighthouse Life in HRM." Undated typescripts.

"Oral histories from Nova Scotia lightkeepers," collected by Chris Mills, 1986–2005.

White, William Chapman. "A Sea Story," in New York Herald Tribune. Undated.

Parliamentary Sessional Papers…

Rules and Instructions for the Guidance of Lighthouse-Keeper and of Engineers in Charge of Steam Fog Alarms in the Dominion of Canada. Ottawa, 1876.

Rules and Instructions for Lightkeepers and Fog Alarm Engineers and Rules Governing Buoys and Beacons. Marine Services. Department of Transport. Ottawa, 1953.

PHOTO CREDITS:

Alice Breau. Pg 117

Canadian Army Photo. Pgs 187, 195, 202

DFO/Canadian Coast Guard. Pgs 47, 116, 163, 170

Nancy Eisener. Pg 205

Anne Flemming. Pg 96

Don Gallagher. Pg 5

Grand Manan Museum. Pg 1

Jim Guptill. Pgs 15, 17, 44, 120, 152, 216

Andrew Hodder. Pg 139

Kathleen Ingersoll. Pgs 48, 50

E. H. Rip Irwin. Pg 184

Faye Lent. Pgs 89, 91

George Locke. Pgs 179, 181

Barry MacDonald. Pg 128

Kathleen Major. Pg 71

Joan McGregor. Pgs 65, 200

Chris Mills. Pgs vi, 9, 13, 14, 19, 20, 24 (bottom), 25 (top), 26–8, 30–1, 70, 73, 87, 93, 95, 103, 109–11, 122, 124, 159, 167, 173, 186, 207, 209, 211, 213, 219, 223–4

National Archives of Canada. Pgs 23 (g-139288), 25 (bottom) (pa-148186)

R. J. Near. Pg 113

Mary Nickerson. Pg 35

NSLPS. Pgs 87, 159, 173

Gorden Schweers. Pg 24 (top)

Geraldine Searles. Pg 135

Muriel Smiley, Pgs 38, 57, 76

Betty June Smith. Pgs 8, 40, 51, 63, 141, 150

J. R. Smith. Pg 53

Sid and Betty June Smith Pgs 36–7, 43, 49, 55, 101, 165, 220–1

Geraldine Stevens. Pgs 67, 84, 86, 218

Anne Wickens. Pgs 81, 136, 226

Ina York. Pg 178

Index